CODES

HOW TO MAKE THEM
AND BREAK THEM!

KJARTAN POSKITT
ILLUSTRATED BY IAN BAKER

FOR YOUNG READERS

Racehorse Publishing books may be purchased in bulk at special
discounts for sales promotion, corporate gifts, fund-raising, or
educational purposes. Special editions can also be created to
specifications. For details, contact the Special Sales Department,
Skyhorse Publishing, 307 West 36th Street, 11th Floor, New York,
NY 10018 or info@skyhorsepublishing.com.

Library of Congress Cataloging-in-Publication Data is available on file.

Racehorse Publishing™ is a pending trademark of Skyhorse Publishing,
Inc.®, a Delaware corporation.

Visit our website at www.skyhorsepublishing.com.

10 9 8 7 6 5 4 3 2 1

Cover design by Michael Short
Cover illustration by Ian Baker

Print ISBN: 978-1-63158-127-4
eBook ISBN: 978-1-63158-128-1

Printed in the United States of America

To my lovely boss "Miss" Lisa Edwards with thanks
for sparing the time to make a guest star
appearance in the last pages of this book.

CONTENTS

A SNEAKY START

As you launch yourself into this extraordinary book, notice that arranged within the main text there are many cunningly concealed kinds of trick messages, only you don't see any just yet.

Hah! Did you spot it? No? We hate to tell you this but you have *already* read a secret message. Yes indeed, a hidden announcement of national importance was sneaked into that first sentence! It uses one of the easiest sorts of codes, but don't worry if you didn't see it as we'll explain it soon.

HAH! THE EARTHLINGS STILL HAVEN'T FINISHED THE INTRODUCTION TO THE BOOK!

WE'VE GOT HERE JUST IN TIME!

WE CAN SNEAK IN AND STEAL ALL THEIR CLEVER CODE IDEAS!

There are hundreds of different ways you can send a message so that it can only be read by the right person, and nearly all of them rely on math. Some codes need extremely murderous math and we'll have a look at those later on, but the code in the first paragraph used some of the simplest math there is. If you want to decode the message, all you need to do is count to 2 but it still fooled you, didn't it?

There are three basic ways of sending secret messages:

- SCRAMBLED (where the order of the letters is mixed up)
- SUBSTITUTED (where each letter is swapped for something else)
- DISGUISED

By now you might have realized that the message in the first sentence is disguised. This means that when you read the sentence, you didn't even realize there was a message there! If we'd started the book by saying XQ3JJF8MZ27 then you might have got a bit suspicious, but as it was, you didn't know there was anything strange happening until we told you.

THERE'S NO MENTION OF US IN THE TEXT SO FAR!

It's time you found out how to decode the first sentence, but do bear in mind that when you see what it says, you needn't worry. It's not as scary as it seems and all is in hand (we hope). Here's that sentence again, but you'll notice that the words are now split into groups of two.

As you – launch yourself – into this – extraordinary book – notice that – arranged within – the main – text there – are many – cunningly concealed – kinds of – trick messages – only you – don't see – any just – yet.

Now just look at the *first letter* of each group. Got the message?

Eeek! It's the evil Gollarks from the planet Zog, but don't panic. Just dive behind the sofa, grab the TV remote and prepare to zap anything green and slimy that approaches. The odd thing about Gollarks is that although they like to invade, causing mayhem and destruction, all it takes is one little push of the TV remote control and *ping* they end up doing whatever program you switched to. Today it's "Gorgeous Gardens."

Special words to know

code:

A code is when you use words or signals to convey special messages. Codes don't have to be secret, for instance MAYDAY is the well-known international code word sent out by ships or planes in trouble. (It comes from the French "m'aider" which means "help me.") So if you get a message from a boat stuck on the rocks saying "MAYDAY," don't immediately start dancing round a striped flagpole waving handkerchiefs. They won't be impressed.

Oi! WE NEED HELP HERE!

BUT WE ALWAYS DO THIS ON MAY DAY.

cryptic message:

This is the general name for any *secret* code—in other words any message that needs decoding before you can understand it. In this book we'll just call cryptic messages "codes" to be simple, but you know what we mean.

cipher:	For substitution messages, the method of swapping the letters for other letters or symbols is called a cipher.
agent:	This is the person you are sending your message to. You like this person.
crackers:	These are the EVIL people such as Professor Fiendish who might get hold of your message and will work tirelessly for days and nights trying to break your code. You don't like crackers, especially as the posh word for them is "cryptanalysts."

plaintext:	This is your uncoded message, and is usually written in lowercase letters.
CODETEXT:	This is your coded message, and is usually written in CAPITAL LETTERS.
algorithm:	This is the general method you've used to encode your messages. It doesn't usually matter if the crackers know this.
key:	This is the little bit of information you need to start decoding a message. You don't want crackers to know this.

The difference between the KEY and the ALGORITHM

The *algorithm* for the first sentence of this book (the one that was coded) is that the hidden message is made up from the first letters of some of the words. Even if the crackers know the algorithm, they don't know which words in the sentence are the important ones.

The *key* describes exactly which words were important. For instance it could be every fourth word, or every fifth word, or perhaps every word before a comma. Crackers who know the algorithm can experiment and try to find the key, and for our first sentence it's so simple they might get it quite quickly.

An obvious algorithm and a coded key

Here's another sort of algorithm that is useless without a key. If you wanted to tell your agent where to find buried treasure, you could print these directions in a newspaper for anybody to read:

20 PACES
NORTH

60 PACES
WEST

10 PACES
SOUTH-EAST
AND START
DIGGING.

NEWS TREASURE ISLAND MAP DISCOVERED.

N
W ⟨⊕⟩ E
S

SKULL ROCK

WELL

TREE

CACTUS

SHED

This is an *algorithm* because it gives plenty of instructions as to what to do, but any crackers would have real problems finding the treasure because they don't know the *key*! In this case, the key would say where your agent has to start walking from. If they guessed wrong and decided to start walking from skull rock, then they'd end up digging a hole in the sea. Ha! Serves them right. The good bit is that as long as the crackers don't know where to start walking, they won't find the treasure.

You could send the key to your agent on a postcard like this:

The key which describes where to start has been coded in the message, just in case the crackers read the newspaper AND they manage to intercept the postcard. Once again we've used the first letters of some of the words on the postcard, but the key to which words we've used is more clever than the one we used before. Why not try to crack it yourself? To give you a clue, hidden in the message on the postcard is one of the places marked on the map! If you give in, the key is below.

Postcard key: Look at all the words ending in "e." Read the first letter of every word that comes immediately afterwards.

The rules of codes

It doesn't matter what sort of code you're using, there are three important rules to remember:

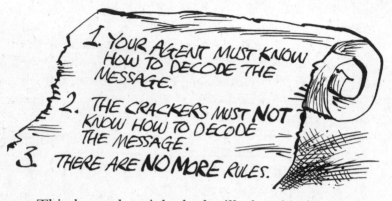

1. YOUR AGENT MUST KNOW HOW TO DECODE THE MESSAGE.

2. THE CRACKERS MUST NOT KNOW HOW TO DECODE THE MESSAGE.

3. THERE ARE NO MORE RULES.

This last rule might look silly but it's important. The whole point of codes is to work in secret; therefore, as long as you can obey rules 1 and 2, then the crazier and more misleading you can make your code and the better it is! As soon as you start obeying rules such as "keywords should only be seven letters long" or "no spelin mistaykes," then you're in danger of being predictable and you'll end up breaking rule 2.

Although this book might look like it's got lots of rules and instructions, they are only guidelines to show you how it all works. If you can think of your own methods and ignore everything here then GOOD FOR YOU. This book just shows and explains how all the codes we know about got invented, but there might be millions more codes being sent around the world that we don't even know about! These codes are probably much better than anything we've got here, but as we don't know about them we can't be sure.

How to make sure you write your codes right!

When you write code out, if you make just one mistake then your whole message could be impossible to decode. What's more it might even help the crackers work out what code you're using! When people sent coded messages in the war, the one thing crackers used to dream of was a message having to be sent twice with a corrected mistake because they could compare them and unravel how the code worked. Therefore it's very important to get your code right first time, so here's what to do:

1 Write your plain message out in small letters along the top of a big piece of paper. Most codes ignore spaces, so leave the spaces out.

2 Work out your coded message and write it underneath. If your encoding takes two or three stages, work out one stage at a time.

3 Finally when you get your completed code, write it out in CAPITAL letters.

4 Now decode it, and make sure it works.

5 Finally copy your coded message out on to the postcard or into the e-mail, or whatever else you're sending it on.

6 It is now traditional to destroy the piece of paper you were working on by eating it. Choose from the following:

- Stuff it in your mouth and chew it up. (Not recommended.)

- Slice into strips, smother in brown sauce, dip into beaten egg, roll in breadcrumbs, and gently fry until brown. Add salt and pepper to taste, then serve with sun-dried tomatoes, moon-dried mushrooms, towel-dried custard, and hairdryer-dried ice. Garnish with basil and rosemary and anybody else you think might taste nice. Serves 4.

- Shove the paper through a shredder and then raid the biscuit tin instead.

DISGUISED MESSAGES

> AHA! THIS LOOKS INTERESTING. WE COULD TRY IT.

Even the best code cracker hasn't a chance if he can't find a message to decode. That's why some people go to great lengths to hide messages in strange and wonderful ways. In ancient times, people used to shave a slave's head, tattoo the message on the bald bit, and then wait for the hair to grow back. The slave would then be sent off to whoever needed the message and have his head shaved again to reveal the message. There was also the Roman general who sent a message back to his base camp written on a small bit of cloth. The cloth was then rolled up very tightly and fed to a messenger's horse! The messenger rode off, but of course if he was stopped the enemy wouldn't find anything. However when he reached the camp, all they had to do was wait until the following morning. . .

We'll leave the old-fashioned ways to the Gollarks. Luckily this is a Murderous Maths book and we've got much easier ways to hide messages!

Needles and haystacks
The first chapter had a few disguised messages where the letters of the plaintext are hidden in a jumble of words. You can easily think of your own algorithm to do this, the only problem is that your coded message might be very long just to get a few secret words across! Did you find the word "cactus" in the coded postcard on page 7? That message was 75 letters long just to disguise six letters. We call this method *needles and haystacks* because picking the correct letters out from all the decoy letters is like finding a needle in a haystack.

If you want to get your message across a bit faster,

you can hide whole words at once. Here's an emergency message you might send to an agent who happens to have a bucket of water handy:

> MY FAT
> DOG PANTS
> WHENEVER
> WE ARE
> PLAYING
> FOOTBALL ON
> THE OLD FIRE
> STATION
> STEPS

The algorithm to decode this message is to divide it into groups of three words, and then read the first word of each group. Eeek!

Another way to hide a message in a jumble of words is to take a page out of a newspaper and stick a pin through the paper underneath the letters you need. When you put the page back, it's very hard to spot the pin holes! All your agent needs to do is take the page out and hold it up to the light and the holes become obvious. (Look at the underlined letters to see how this works!)

Binary codes

So far we've hardly used any math and so regular Murderous Maths fans will be getting a bit twitchy. Take a deep breath then, because now we're going to use binary numbers to disguise a message. Binary numbers only use the digits 0 and 1, and if you wanted to write the number 6 in binary, you'd put 110. (And if you wanted to write one hundred and ten in binary, you'd put 1101110.) The good news is that you don't need to understand binary itself, but if you want to it's all explained in *Numbers: The Key to the Universe*.

The first thing to do is to turn your message into binary, so you get a load of 1s and 0s. After that you can disguise the 1s and 0s in all sorts of different ways. The lovely thing about these messages is that they can really confuse crackers. This short binary message actually says *yes*:

NO DEFiNITeLY nOt

You might be suspicious at the range of capitals and small letters, and you'd be right! This next message also says *yes* and it uses exactly the same encoding system, but the disguise is slightly better:

No definitely *not*

If you look carefully you'll see that the four letters that were small in the first message (i, e, n, and t) are now in *italics*. The secret message is hidden in the arrangement of plain and italic letters and so the fun part is that it doesn't matter what the letters themselves are. Here's another message coded the same way. Can you guess what it says?

Absolu*te*ly no *way*

Wrong again. It also says *yes* and so does this one:
aaaaa*a*aaa*a*aa*a*a

We've encoded the word *yes* using a *five-bit binary code*. To decode a message, you first break it into sections of five letters. Then you write 1 under every normal letter and 0 under every italic letter. You get this:

N o d e f   *i* n i t *e*   l y *n o t*
1 1 1 1 1   0 1 1 1 0   1 1 0 1 0

The code is hidden in these five digit numbers containing 1s and 0s. There are 32 different ways you can write out five 1s and 0s, and each of them can represent a different number or letter. Here's the system we've used:

00000 = 0	01010 = a	10101 = m
00001 = 1	01011 = b	10110 = n
00010 = 2	01100 = c	10111 = o
00011 = 3	01101 = d	11000 = p/q
00100 = 4	01110 = e	11001 = r
00101 = 5	01111 = f	11010 = s
00110 = 6	10000 = g	11011 = t
00111 = 7	10001 = h	11100 = u
01000 = 8	10010 = i	11101 = v
01001 = 9	10011 = j/k	11110 = w/x
	10100 = l	11111 = y/z

You'll see that we've let some binary numbers (e.g. 10011) represent two letters. This is because with five-bit binary we don't have enough numbers for all the 26 letters and 10 digits. As it's the more unusual letters that are paired up, when you decode the message it should be obvious enough which letter you need.

The first group of five digits was 11111, so this represents y or z. The next group was 01110 so that represented e and the final group was 11010 that gives you the s.

Of course you don't have to use the binary code we've seen here. You and your agent can set up your own five-bit code and use the 32 different binary numbers to represent anything you like. Suppose you didn't need the digits 0–9, you could give each of the 26 letters a different number and that would leave you with 6 numbers for special words or phrases, such as "No" or "Get here immediately" or "Darling, I love you passionately until the end of time."

There are a lot of reasons for *not* using binary code:

- If you're going to use italics, you almost certainly have to assemble your message with a computer. This could be a bit awkward if you're wandering through an enemy campsite disguised in a cow outfit and just clutching a pencil and paper.

- If you miss out just one digit, it will be impossible to read any of the message that comes after it.
- It takes ages to write anything more than a few words.

However there is one job this sort of code is really good for. If you are sending a scrambled or substitution message, sometimes it's useful to be able to hide the key to the code in the message. (The key can often be just one word or even one letter!) Therefore, you might arrange with your agent that the key is hidden with binary code in the first few letters of the message!

So if cAPitAl LETteRs MeAN oNE aND THE sMALL LetTErs MEaN ZErO THIS IS WHaT wE THINk oF bINaRY CoDe.

Anyone squirting custard is idiotic

Although binary code is a bit tedious for people to use, computers absolutely love it. In fact they love it so much that they tend to use eight digit numbers rather than just the five digits we've got here. This eight-bit code is called "ASCII," which stands for Anyone Squirting Custard Is Idiotic.

(It also stands for American Standard Code for Information Interchange but that's a bit boring.)

When you push a key on a computer keyboard, it sends a binary code into the computer. In total there are 256 different combinations of eight 1s and 0s, so the keyboard can send a different code for all the letters, numbers, commas, and #@+£%^ signs.

If you push *a*, it sends 01100001 and if you push *shift a*, (in other words you want to write "A") it sends 01000001. The numbers from zero to nine all start with 0011, so zero = 00110000 and one = 00110001 and two = 00110010 and so on.

Any codes that start 0000 or 0001 are a bit different. These are *control* codes that don't represent something that can be printed. Most of them don't come off the keyboard, they just run around inside the computer giving it strange computer-ish instructions such as *line feed* or *synchronous idle*. Sadly they don't have sensible instructions such as *order pizza* or *let the cat out*, in fact there's only one of these codes that is any fun: 00000111 = *bell*.

In old-fashioned teletypers and printers, this code would make a little bell *ping*. These days 00000111 might prod your computer into

making a sad little beep noise, but if you're lucky it might dash outside and ring your neighbor's doorbell then run away. Ho ho.

One advantage of having a message in binary code is that computers can then go to work on it and encode it in very complicated ways, as we'll see when we get to page 76.

Unwritten messages
Another advantage of binary code is that it's good for messages that are not written down.

SOUND You could send a message using sound by having two different whistles; the higher note means 0 and the lower note means 1.

SMELL Professor Fiendish has been sending binary code using two lunch boxes marked 1 and 0. The 1 box contains old kipper yogurt and the 0 box has vintage green cheese sandwiches. By cleverly opening and closing the boxes, he can send messages to his pet pig Truffles.

LIGHT   You could send a message in binary at
         night to an agent over the road using
         your bedroom light. If you turn your light
         on and off once very quickly, that could
         mean "0" and if you turn it on and leave
         it for a second then turn it off, that would
         mean "1." You could also leave the light
         off for a longer gap after every five
         flashes to show when a letter had
         finished. And if your agent sees the light
         has gone off for a long time, that will
         mean you've blown a fuse.

Morse code

This is the more usual way of sending messages with flashy lights. It takes a bit more practice than binary, but when you get used to it, it's a lot quicker because the more common letters only use one or two flashes. The letters and numbers are represented with a selection of short and long flashes like this:

A · -	B - · · ·	C - · - ·	D - · ·	E ·
F · · - ·	G - - ·	H · · · ·	I · ·	J · - - -
K - · -	L · - · ·	M - -	N - ·	O - - -
P · - - ·	Q - - · -	R · - ·	S · · ·	T -
U · · -	V · · · -	W · - -	X - · · -	Y - · - -
Z - - · ·				
0 - - - - -	1 · - - - -	2 · · - - -	3 · · · - -	4 · · · · -
5 · · · · ·	6 - · · · ·	7 - - · · ·	8 - - - · ·	9 - - - - ·
Full stop · - · - · -		Comma - - · · - -		? · · - - · ·

(Since e-mails got popular there is even a code for @, which is · - - · - ·)

Morse code is quite well known, so usually you would encode a message first using one of the substitution or scrambling methods we'll see later on.

SCRAMBLING CODES

You can encode messages by changing the order that the letters come in. Down at the Last Chance Saloon, the card hostess Riverboat Lil often did this to disguise messages, especially when Brett Shuffler was on the lookout for easy money.

24

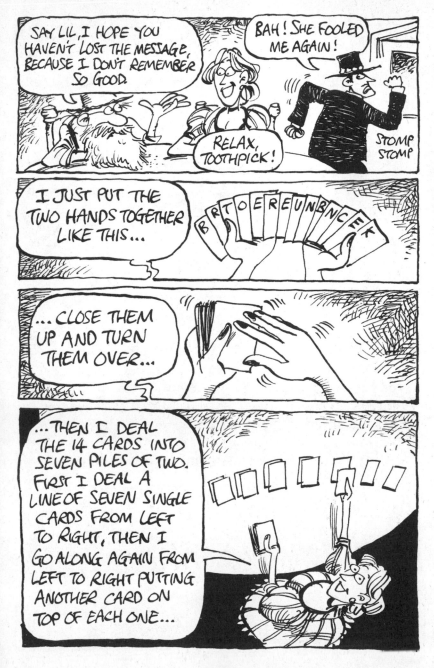

This is one of the best known ways of scambling a message, although if you don't want to deal cards there's an easier way. It's called the *rail fence* method because in the old days rail fences used to have a nice zig-zag top to them. Imagine you write your message along the top, and every second letter sits on a spike of the fence.

You remove all the letters on the fence and you're left with BRTOERE. After that you write in all the letters you removed: UNBNCEK. Put them together and you get BRTOEREUNBNCEK. When Lil dealt the cards out into two piles she was doing the same thing—in other words she was removing every second card and putting them into a separate pile. To decode a rail fence message you have to write it out like this:

```
B   R   T   O   E   R   E
  U   N   B   N   C   E   K
```

and slot the letters back together. When Lil dealt the cards into seven piles of two, she was just putting the cards she removed back into their original places. (Needless to say, to do this with a pack of cards, you have to be as good at dealing as Lil and that's *very* good.)

STICK AROUND AND I'LL SHOW YOU HOW TO DO IT!

The rail fence method only splits your letters into two groups, but if you want to make things harder for the crackers, you can split your letters into more groups. The way to do it is to write the letters in a grid so that they read across:

```
y   o   u   r   g   r   i   d
c   a   n   b   e   a   n   y
s   i   z   e   y   o   u   l
i   k   e   f   o   r   t   h
e   m   e   s   s   a   g   e
```

27

To encode your message, you just read *down* the columns one at a time! Here you get YCSIE OAIKM UNZEE RBEFS GEYOS RAORA INUTG DYLHE. As the grid we used had eight columns going across, we've broken the letters up into eight groups! Just to make things more confusing, we'll move the spaces around: YCS IEOAI KMU NZEE RB EFSGEYO SRA ORAI NU T GDYLHE. Now the crackers can't tell how many columns were in the grid (but don't forget to let your agent know!)

How to scramble messages by dealing cards

You can use as many or as few cards as you like, but the total number of cards you use must not be prime, in other words it must be a number that will divide up neatly. When Lil scrambled up Toothpick's message she used 14 cards, which divides up into 7 × 2. When she scrambled the message she dealt two piles of seven cards each, then to unscamble it she dealt seven piles of two.

If you want to practice, try using 12 cards: Ace, 2, 3, 4, 5, 6, 7, 8, 9, 10, Jack, and Queen. Twelve divides up into 3 × 4, so first you can scramble them up by dealing them into *three* piles, and then unscamble them by dealing them into *four* piles. Here's how it goes:

- First, put the cards in order from Ace–Queen.

- Turn them face down and deal them into THREE piles. Put a card on each pile in turn as if you're dealing to three people.

- Put the piles together. The pile on top should be the pile on which the last card was dealt.

- Turn the whole pack over and fan them out. You'll see the cards are in a scrambled-up order!

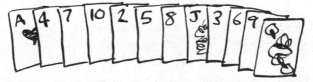

- Turn the pack face down, then deal them into FOUR piles.

- Put the piles together in the same way as before.
- Turn the whole pack over, fan them out and look. . .

THE CARDS ARE BACK IN THE RIGHT ORDER.

WELL SHOOT MA BOOT!

You can try this with other numbers of cards. For instance if you use 40 cards, remember 5 × 8 = 40. So first deal them into five piles, and then deal them into eight piles!

Other methods of scrambling

If you want to start scrambling up a message that you haven't finished writing, you can't use a grid or rail fence method but there are lots of other ways you can do it. How about this:

- Break your message into groups of three letters.
- Reverse each group of three letters.
- Put it together again!

WE MIGHT TRY THIS LATER ON!

OOOH!

This message was encoded this way, so you can try to decode it:

IHTSIS CINNAE AEDJYS

You'll notice that when the message was coded, an extra letter was put on the end to complete the group of three and make it neat. Also the finished message was broken into groups of six letters just for fun. Why not? So long as you could decode it, that's all that matters, remember rule 3 on page 8: *there are no more rules.*

Scramble talk

You can have fun imagining your message is written out backwards, and saying it out loud! If you and your agent practice this, other people will have no idea what you are talking about. "Good afternoon" would sound like "Noon Ret Fah Dug." This is really handy if you suspect you're being overheard by aliens.

Scramble strips

Back in ancient times, people used to write scrambled messages on long strips of paper. When the strip was laid out flat, all that could be seen was a row of meaningless letters, but when the strip was wrapped around a pole with exactly the right thickness, the message would suddenly become obvious! Over the years, this method was adapted and used in many clever and cunning ways. Here's one as described in an old police report.

City: Chicago, Illinois, USA
Place: Central Mail Office, City Square
Date: 7 November 1929
Time: 9:15 am

"Sorry sir," said the little man wearing a waistcoat and watch chain behind the armored desk. "No letter here for a Mr James Boccelli. I checked twice already."

The three shady men glared through the grill at the mail clerk. The slim man and the man in the black suit stood in front of a very large man who was as wide as the other two put together. It was the large man that spoke.

"But Jimmy ordered the security uniforms weeks ago!" said Porky Boccelli.

"Shhh!" whispered the slim man putting his finger to his lips. "This is supposed to be a secret plan."

"You sure there's no letter for my brother James?" asked Blade Boccelli, his hands twitching angrily inside the pockets of his black jacket.

"No letter," said the clerk. "But Boccelli . . . ? Wait right there, I think I saw something arrive in the packages."

The clerk disappeared through a doorway into a large room full of sacks and baskets. The three men turned to each other.

"A package?" said Blade. "Surely Stitch hasn't posted seven uniforms?"

"The plan was that he'd let us know when he had them ready and I'd collect," said One-Finger Jimmy.

The clerk returned with a triumphant smile on his face and a small parcel in his hand. "James Boccelli!" he said. "Sign here please."

One Finger Jimmy reached inside his jacket for a pen, but when he looked at the counter again there was no sign of the clerk. This came as no surprise to Jimmy. Whenever he reached inside his jacket, people had a habit of ducking behind counters, throwing themselves out of windows or hiding behind huge vases of flowers, just in case he was reaching for a gun. Jimmy might only have one finger, but everyone knew how fast it could pull a trigger.

By the time they had got out into the street, the three men were already ripping the paper from the parcel that was no bigger than a chocolate box. They would have been very surprised if it had contained seven uniforms, but when they opened it, they were even more surprised.

"A belt?" gasped Blade. "Just one old leather belt? How can we disguise ourselves with one belt and rob a bank?"

"It's a very long belt," said Jimmy passing it to his larger brother. "Maybe it's for you, Porky."

"I never had a belt that went all the way round me before," said the big man wistfully. "I always had to wear suspenders. Let me try it."

As the big man fumbled around his waistline, Blade picked a small card from the wrapping. It had just two words on it: *For Dolly*.

"I don't believe this," said Blade. "It must mean for Dolly Snowlips!"

The others gasped. Dolly was a real dainty dresser. Her hats, heels and handbags were all picked from the city's classiest boutiques. Somehow they couldn't see her wearing this glorified baggage strap. What's more. . .

"I wouldn't dare give this to Dolly!" said Blade. "If she thought this belt was supposed to be her size, she'd rip us to shreds and feed the pieces to rats."

Porky had carefully threaded the belt through all his belt loops and to his delight, not only could he do it up, there was even a bit spare.

"Looks good to me," said Blade.

"Looks good to me too," agreed Jimmy. "In fact anything that holds up Porky's pants looks good to me. I'd hate to see them fall down."

But Blade wasn't listening.

Instead he was examining a mixed-up cluster of letters etched on to the leather in black ink.

"Hey Jimmy!" said Blade. "Maybe it's some sort of coded message about the uniforms?"

"But how do we read it?" said Jimmy. "The only clue is that card."

They all gulped. Maybe they had to give the belt to Dolly after all, so that's what they did. Being a Thursday, they found her perched on a stool in the ice cream shop, and as they suspected, when they passed the belt over, she wasn't best pleased.

"Of course it's not my size," said Dolly taking an indignant slurp from a peppermint and peanut cream fizz. "I'm a size NYM and have been for years."

"NYM?" asked Blade. "What size is that?"

"Never You Mind!" snapped Dolly.

"So why would Stitch put a card in saying it's for Dolly?" asked Porky.

"Stitch Fuldrag?" Dolly was suddenly interested. She swiveled around on the stool to face them, her thin eyebrows arched in curiosity. "Stitch has known me and my size for years. He's the sharpest needleman in the city. Maybe I should try it on."

Dolly hopped down from the stool and tried the belt that wrapped around her waist exactly three times. At first it seemed pointless, but then. . .

"Hey!" gasped Blade, "look at it sideways!"

To be continued. . .

SUBSTITUTION CODES

It's Christmas time at Fogsworth Manor, and for once Rodney Bounder has bought a few presents for other people. The Duchess, the Colonel, and Lord Binkiebott Marmalade Fogsworth are quite overcome with surprise.

It looks like Binkie is in luck, because his full name of "Lord Binkiebott Marmalade Fogsworth" has 32 letters, exactly the same number as the letters on the label.

Rodney has used a very simple substitution code. For every letter of the names, he has written down the letter *that comes before it* in the alphabet. Therefore to decode the names and find out who gets which present, you just work out the letter that comes *after* each letter on the labels. On the label attached to the Duchess's present, the "C" becomes "d" and "T" becomes "u" and so on. (Remember that it helps to put CODETEXT in CAPITALS and plaintext in small letters.)

What a rotten trick, and when you decode the long label you'll see why! If you haven't decoded it yet, then wait until you've read the next section.

How to make code strips

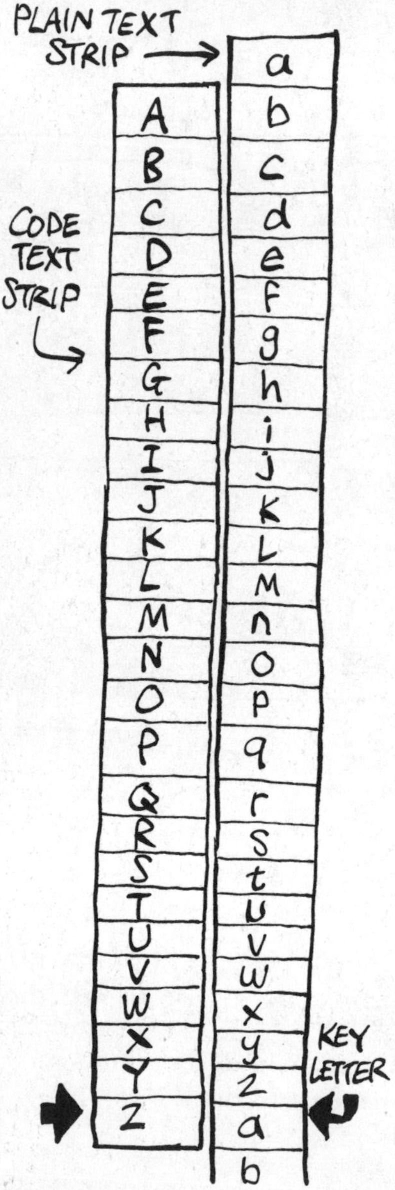

PLAIN TEXT STRIP →

CODE TEXT STRIP ↓→

KEY LETTER

There's a very simple gadget you can make to help encode and decode messages like Rodney's labels. All you need are two thin strips of paper, one of which is twice as long as the other. To make things simple, the long one should be 52 cm and the shorter one 26 cm, and both of them should be marked off in centimeters. The long strip is your plaintext strip, so you should start at one end and fill in the spaces by writing the whole alphabet out twice in little letters.

The shorter strip is the CODETEXT strip. To do an easy code like the one Rodney used, you just write out the alphabet in CAPITAL letters in the spaces. Now you lie the strips alongside each other. If you put A on the CODETEXT strip next to the *a* at the end of the plaintext strip, then the other letters should match up all the way along to Z and z. Here comes the clever bit. You slide the CODETEXT strip along one place so that the Z is now next to the other *a* in the middle of the plaintext strip.

Whatever letter represents *a* is the *key*, so these strips are now set with the key = Z. This is the key to decoding Rodney's labels! The Duchess's coded label started with C, so find the CODETEXT letter C, and you'll see the plaintext letter next to it is *d*.

If you're clever and want to make something a bit neater, you can make a pair of code wheels. These are two circles of paper; the smaller one has the plaintext letters *a–z* written round the edge, and the bigger one has the CODETEXT letters A–Z written round the edge. You fix them with a pin through the centers so that the small wheel can be rotated. Hint—when you write your CODETEXT letters, use a pencil. This is so you can rub them out and change the order when you find out about keywords later on.

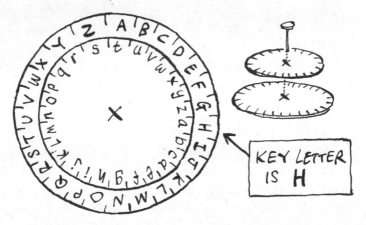

KEY LETTER IS H

Making your own substitution codes

If you want to send a coded message to an agent, you both need a set of code strips. The fun part is that you can choose any one of 25 completely different codes. All you do is change the key, which can be any letter apart from A. (If the key letter was A, then A would = a and B = b and C = c, etc. Your secret messages wouldn't be very secret.)

The ancient Roman Julius Caesar sent lots of messages by shifting the alphabet along and so this process is called a *Caesar shift*. Most of the time Julius shifted the alphabet along three places, which means the key letter would be D. If he had been using code strips, he would have lined them up so that D was next to a, and then sent a message such as:

LORYH VSURX WVLQF XVWDU G

(You'll notice that to confuse things even more, people don't usually bother leaving the normal gaps between words in codes. Instead they just break them up into equal groups of letters.)

TIP! When decoding messages like this, to save a bit of time, when you know what a letter represents (e.g. L = i) put it in wherever it appears. So with this message after you've worked out L O and R, you'll have this:

LORYH VSURX WVLQF XVWDU G
i l o   o   i

This system is easy for you and your agent but unfortunately it's also easy for the crackers who will happily try out the 25 different code possibilities until they stumble on your message. It won't take long; they might just start with key = B and try it on the first few letters. If the results obviously don't make sense, they'll try key = C and then key = D and so on until they get it.

IT ONLY TAKES ME A COUPLE OF MINUTES!

You can try code cracking yourself. Here are three messages all done with different key letters. Time yourself and see how fast you can decode all three!

1 wKLvR QHLVH DVB

2 LyOes TDTDP LDJEZ Z

3 GZOnH VFZDO CVMYZ M

(Incidentally the first five letters of each message have been coded with binary code to hide the key letter! Capitals = 1 and small letters = 0. See page 16.)

The key letters are 1-D 2-L 3-V.

43

Keywords and killer codes

If you want to get a lot more than 25 different codes, you just need to change the order of the letters on your CODETEXT strip. So far we've only seen the CODETEXT letters in alphabetical order, but if you shuffle them round, every different order of letters produces a different code! You can work out how many different ways there are of writing out 26 letters by multiplying $26 \times 25 \times 24 \times 23 \times \ldots \times 3 \times 2 \times 1$ and the answer is: 403,291,461,126,605,635,584,000,000. Can you imagine how long it would take a cracker to try them all out? Yippee!

Of course your agent must know what order your 26 CODETEXT letters are in, and there's an easy way of arranging this. You use *keywords*.

● Choose some keywords you'll remember.

● Write out the keywords then cross out any repeated letters.

SAUSAGEROLLS

● Write out the letters that remain without any gaps.

SAUGEROL

● Now write in all the rest of the letters of the alphabet in order. You start with the letter that comes after the last letter of your key. Here Binkie's key finishes with L, so the next letter is M then N then P (we've already used O so we miss that out) and so on. When you get to Z, you continue with A and carry on until you've written out all 26 letters.

SAUGEROLMNPQTVWXYZBCDFHIJK

This is how your letters go on your CODETEXT strip, and the clever bit is that your agent only has to remember "sausage rolls" to know the exact order. And just to stir things up a bit more, we'll add in a key letter. . .

P FOR PARTY!

. . . and you can encode your message. Remember that the key letter P on the CODESTRIP goes next to the letter *a* and here's what you get. . .

q r s t u v w x y z a b c d e f g h i j k l m n o p
S A U G E R O L M N P Q T V W X Y Z B C D F H I J K

So long as your agent knows the keywords and key letter they can decode the message, but for anyone else it will be *very* difficult!

46

Secret ways to send keywords

One huge advantage of keywords is that you can change your code very quickly. All you need to do is let your agent know what the new keywords are, but obviously you should do this as secretly as possible.

- You could write the keywords on paper with invisible ink that you can make from all sorts of different things. A few years ago you were allowed to try lemon juice. You could stick a cocktail stick into a slice of lemon, then draw a few squiggles of juice on a piece of paper. You wouldn't be able to see it, but if you heated it up by holding it near a candle or putting it in the oven it would go brown! Sadly these days you can't do it unless you are wearing safety gloves and goggles, you have two responsible adults supervising you, the emergency services are on standby and the council inspectors have issued you with a hazard assessment certificate. Still, better to be safe, eh?

WITHOUT ADULT SUPERVISION   WITH ADULT SUPERVISION

- If you're posting a coded message, you could hide your keywords written in tiny letters under the stamp on the envelope!
- If you wanted to change your keywords every day, you can arrange with your agent that the keywords

are the first three words to appear on page 6 of *The Daily Slur*. So when you send your message, you have a look at that day's newspaper, write down the agreed words and off you go.

Computer tip

If you've got a computer and you've got a really long message you want to put into code, there's a neat way of doing it. First of all, you choose how everything is going to substitute. Here's a basic CODETEXT just using the key letter = M:

a b c d e f g h i j k l m n o p q r s t u v w x y z
M N O P Q R S T U V W X Y Z A B C D E F G H I J K L

You want to turn a = M and m = Y and y = K and so on. Write this out on a piece of paper so you can look at it while you're working on your message.

- On your computer, start up any word program. The basic "Notepad" program on a PC is as good as anything and it doesn't try to correct your spelling, which can be a real pain when you're writing codes!

- Type out your message in lowercase letters. It's as well to save a copy of it too in case you mess up the encoding process! This is the longest part of the job.
- On the "edit" or "tools" menu use "find/replace." You're going to swap each plain letter for a code letter, but before you do, ensure that "match case" is on. This makes sure you only swap little or capital letters, but not both at once.
- It's time to swap your first letter, so put "a" in the "find" box and "M" in the replace box and then try it. All the "as" should turn into "Ms." Swap all the other letters into code the same way.
- Print it out or copy it and e-mail it!

Don't forget about using "match case." Otherwise you'll start by making all the "as" into "Ms," then later on when you turn the "ms" into "Ys," all the "Ms" will turn into "Ys" too. The word "jam" will become jYY. Of course if you did this for the whole alphabet, you'd end up with a message that was just pages and pages of the same letter. There is some good news though. . .

Moving on

For most of us living our normal lives, this is as far as we need to take substitution codes. After all, using keywords gives us way more than *400 million million million million* possibilities, so guessing is going to be as near impossible as anything can get. This sort of code was used in various ways for thousands of years before anybody worked out how to crack these messages, and when they did find a way, it wasn't easy!

Frequency analysis

It was around the ninth century AD that Arab language scholars realized that some letters of their alphabet were much more common than others, so if somebody sent a long coded message, one way to start guessing at the answer was to see which letters turned up the most. In Arabic, the letters *a* and *l* are the most common, so if a coded message had a lot of letter Js in it, they would guess that J = *a* and if there were a lot of letter Ys then maybe Y = *l*. They would then try guessing at some of the other common letters to see if any whole words appeared. If it didn't work, they'd start again and maybe try it the other way round making J = *l* and Y = *a* and so on.

Of course this method relies on clever guesswork, but it's the basis of how substitution codes are cracked today, and now that we have computers to do the guessing, it only takes seconds!

BAH! I WISH THEY'D HURRY UP AND INVENT COMPUTERS.

In the English language, *e* is by far the most commonly used letter. It occurs 12.7% of the time—in other words if you have a message that is 1,000 letters long, then about 127 of the letters will be *e*. After that, *t* occurs 9.1% of the time, and then *a* occurs 8.2% and so on. (This book has almost 14,000 *e*s, about 10,000 *t*s and 8,000 *a*s so we're very close to the average.) Here's a table showing the percentage that each letter appears:

e	12.7	**d**	4.3	**p**	1.9
t	9.1	**l**	4.0	**b**	1.5
a	8.2	**u**	2.8	**v**	1.0
o	7.5	**c**	2.8	**k**	0.8
i	7.0	**m**	2.4	**x**	0.2
n	6.7	**w**	2.4	**j**	0.2
s	6.3	**f**	2.2	**q**	0.1
h	6.1	**y**	2.0	**z**	0.1
r	6.0	**g**	2.0		

The least used letters are *q* and *z*, both of which only turn up about one time in a thousand letters unless you're writing to Queen Zelda of Zanzibar quickly requesting quality prizes for a quirky quiz while quietly queuing for the zoo to see the squirrels and zebras.

If you have a nice long coded message, you would start by finding the most common letter and swapping it for "e." You then look for the next most common letter and swap it for "t", and then find the next most common letter and swap it for "a" and so on. Once you've swapped six or seven letters, it should become obvious whether you might get a proper message or whether it's just going to be rubbish and you need to try again. Of course, sometimes there will be more *t*s than *e*s or there might be a ridiculous amount of *f*s, but if you are trying to guess what each coded letter stands for, this method gives you a start.

Naturally this can go wrong, in particular if you only try to work out what a short paragraph is saying.

Crackers would hate that sentence because it has no letter "e"! If you tried substituting "e" for the most common letter, or the second most common letter, or even the third most common letter, you wouldn't get anywhere. Normally the letter "e" turns up in about 60% of English words, but in French it turns up in over 80% of words. In 1969, a French author called Georges Perec was challenged to write a whole book without a single letter "e." The result was called *La*

Disparition and an American called Gilbert Adair translated it into English still without any "e"s! Gilbert used all sorts of tricks such as instead of writing "*three* girls" he'd put "*a trio of* girls." Incidentally, Georges once wrote a story of 466 words and the only vowel he used was "a." That would *really* fool the crackers!

How to make substitution codes more secure

There are several things you can try without giving yourself or your agent too much of a headache.

Disguise the common letters
You can do this by making your plaintext code strip like this:

```
a a b c d e e f g h ij k l m n o p q r  s  t
A B C D E F G H I  J  K L M N O P Q R S  T
t  u  v wx yz 2
U V W X Y Z
```

Of course you can use a keyword and scramble up the CODETEXT strip too, but for now we'll keep it as it is. You'll notice that there are two letters A and B that both represent *a*. There are also two letters for *e* and two letters for *t*. We only use one letter for *i/j*, *p/q*, *w/x* and *y/z*. This will make it much harder for crackers to spot the most common letters. There's also a number "2" at the end! This indicates a double letter, so if you wanted to spell the word "bookkeeper" you'd write it as "bo2k2e2per." When double letters appear, it helps crackers guess what they might be, so hiding them confuses things even more.

Use strange symbols

You can make up a range of odd little drawings or symbols rather than code letters, e.g. ✳= a and ◎= b, and so on. This looks nice and confusing but the problem is that they can be tricky to remember, and when you write them out, you have to take real care that they are clear.

Use more than 26 code letters and symbols

Why not? As well as using A–Z, you can also use 0–9 plus any other odd little signs you like the look of. Computer keyboards are full of cute little things that you never get to use, so now's your chance.

Your extra symbols can mean whatever you like and quite often it's handy if they replace whole words or useful phrases like these:

& = you
% = today
> = come here
@ = call me
+ = emergency
~ = pepperoni pizza
} = dry clean only
! = please send me £1,000,000 immediately

We've already seen how it can be useful to have a symbol for a double letter, but another thing that fools crackers is to have some "null" symbols which mean nothing! You just put a few in wherever you like and let the crackers worry about them for no reason.

Mary Queen of Scots' code
In 1586 when Queen Elizabeth I had Mary Queen of Scots locked up in Chartley Hall in Staffordshire, Mary's supporters tried to organize getting Elizabeth assassinated and replacing her with Mary. This was so dangerous that they used to send Mary messages from London written in a code that used about 60 different symbols  to represent letters, words, names, and double letters. She even had four null symbols. These messages were carried up and down the country by a priest called Gilbert Gifford, and to make sure the guards didn't see them, they were smuggled into the hall hidden in the

stoppers of beer barrels. Mary was so sure that the messages were safe that she wrote some very dangerous things in them.

Unfortunately, what Mary's team didn't know is that Gifford was a spy! Every message he took was copied and given to a man called Thomas Phelippes. Even though Thomas was a quiet, weedy little man who you've never heard of, he is just the sort of person who gets to star in Murderous Maths books because he managed to crack Mary's code and so changed the course of British history!

Thomas used frequency analysis on her early messages and gradually worked out which symbols represented words, which were letters and which were "nulls." Within months Elizabeth's team could read everything Mary was writing and she ended up having her head chopped off, which was all very nasty. It took a few big swipes of the axe and then a bit of sawing to finish the job. Urghhh! Let's quickly move on. . .

Switching codes

If we don't want our heads chopped off like Mary, then we've got to make things harder for the crackers like Thomas Phelippes. The weakness of codes like Mary's is that as soon as Thomas knew what a symbol meant, it always meant the same thing. For example, when he knew that 8 represented the letter y, then *every* time he saw an 8 he knew it meant y.

What would be much better is a system where the code keeps changing with every letter! There's a simple way of doing this with your two basic code strips on page 40. Choose a key letter to start with—

in this case we'll use D, so you start off your strips lined up with D next to *a* like this:

```
u  v  w  x  y  z  a  b  c  d  e  f  g  h  i  j
         A  B  C  D  E  F  G  H  I  J  K  L  M
k  l  m  n  o  p  q  r  s  t  u  v  w  x  y  z
N  O  P  Q  R  S  T  U  V  W  X  Y  Z
```

Now we'll find something really secret to put into code. Let's visit Pongo McWhiffy's Deluxe Burger Bar and see what his mystery ingredient for cheeseburgers is.

IT'S CHEESE!

Gosh! We'd never have suspected that. We thought he used the insides of old tennis shoes. Anyway let's see what happens when we encode the word **cheese**.

Check the strips to see what the first letter should be. Next to *c* is F, so write that down.

Before you encode the second letter, you move the code strip one place to the left so the key letter becomes E.

```
u v w x y z a b c d e f g h i j k l m n o p q r s t u v w x
  A B C D E F G H I J K L M N O P Q R S T U V W X Y Z
```

Now we see what letter we need for *h* and it's L.

Again we move the strips one place. . .

u v w x y z a b c d e f g h i j k l m n o p q r s t u v w x
A B C D E F G H I J K L M N O P Q R S T U V W X Y Z

. . . and we find that for *e* we need the letter J.

If you keep going, the word "cheese" becomes FLJKZM. Here's the good bit— "cheese" has three *e*s but in FLJKZM they have all turned into different letters!

This is the basis of a very powerful code system invented by a Frenchman called Blaise de Vigenere at about the same time that Mary was in trouble. He laid out a table of plaintext and 26 lines of CODETEXT like this:

```
   a b c d e f g h i j k l m n o p q r s t u v w x y z
 1 B C D E F G H I J K L M N O P Q R S T U V W X Y Z A
 2 C D E F G H I J K L M N O P Q R S T U V W X Y Z A B
 3 D E F G H I J K L M N O P Q R S T U V W X Y Z A B C
 4 E F G H I J K L M N O P Q R S T U V W X Y Z A B C D
 5 F G H I J K L M N O P Q R S T U V W X Y Z A B C D E
 6 G H I J K L M N O P Q R S T U V W X Y Z A B C D E F
 7 H I J K L M N O P Q R S T U V W X Y Z A B C D E F G
 8 I J K L M N O P Q R S T U V W X Y Z A B C D E F G H
 9 J K L M N O P Q R S T U V W X Y Z A B C D E F G H I
10 K L M N O P Q R S T U V W X Y Z A B C D E F G H I J
11 L M N O P Q R S T U V W X Y Z A B C D E F G H I J K
12 M N O P Q R S T U V W X Y Z A B C D E F G H I J K L
13 N O P Q R S T U V W X Y Z A B C D E F G H I J K L M
14 O P Q R S T U V W X Y Z A B C D E F G H I J K L M N
15 P Q R S T U V W X Y Z A B C D E F G H I J K L M N O
16 Q R S T U V W X Y Z A B C D E F G H I J K L M N O P
17 R S T U V W X Y Z A B C D E F G H I J K L M N O P Q
18 S T U V W X Y Z A B C D E F G H I J K L M N O P Q R
19 T U V W X Y Z A B C D E F G H I J K L M N O P Q R S
20 U V W X Y Z A B C D E F G H I J K L M N O P Q R S T
21 V W X Y Z A B C D E F G H I J K L M N O P Q R S T U
22 W X Y Z A B C D E F G H I J K L M N O P Q R S T U V
23 X Y Z A B C D E F G H I J K L M N O P Q R S T U V W
24 Y Z A B C D E F G H I J K L M N O P Q R S T U V W X
25 Z A B C D E F G H I J K L M N O P Q R S T U V W X Y
26 A B C D E F G H I J K L M N O P Q R S T U V W X Y Z
```

Notice that the first letter on each row represents *a*, so it is the key letter for that line of CODETEXT. When we encoded "cheese," we started by using line 3 (which has key letter = D), and then we kept moving down one line at a time as we encoded each letter.

TIP! To make it easier to use this table, write the plaintext alphabet along the edge of a straight strip of paper, making it exactly the same size as the top row of the table. All you need to do is position your plaintext strip underneath the row of CODETEXT you're using and you can quickly read off the letters you need. This helps a lot when you're using the lines towards the bottom of the table.

KEY LETTERS

MOVE SO THAT "a" IS UNDER THE KEY LETTER YOU NEED.

A bit of practice

Warning: We're about to learn how to make and crack some of the toughest codes ever invented! If you really want to understand it all, you should first practice using Blaise de Vigenere's table, and get used to how the CODETEXT, plaintext, and key letters are all linked together.

Here are some examples:

- If the key letter is P and the plaintext letter is *m*, then what's the CODETEXT letter? You look along row 15 (the one that starts with P) until you reach the column under *m*. The answer is B.
- If the key letter is F and the CODETEXT letter is L, what is the plaintext letter? Look along row 5 until you get to L, and the plaintext letter at the top of the column is *g*.
- If the CODETEXT is K and the plaintext is *r*, what is the key letter? Find the column with *r* on top, look down until you get to K, then look at the first letter on that row—which is T.
- If the key letter is A, then all plaintext and CODETEXT letters match! (So *a* = A and *b* = B, etc.)

Making it even tougher

If you encode your message by moving down the table one line at a time, a clever cracker might realize what you've done. Never mind, this is only the start. What really makes things tough is if you use the code lines in a funny order. What you do is choose one or more keywords. . .

. . .and then we'll think of an important message to encode:

The first thing to do is to write out the message and then write the keyword above it lots of times so that the letters line up like this:

keyword: CH I P S CH I P S CH I P S CH I P S C
plaintext: i l o v e v e r o n i c a g u m f l o s s
CODETEXT:

The letters in CHIPS will tell you which row of the table you should use to translate each letter of your plaintext. When you translate the first "i" the letter above it is C so check the table and you'll see row 2 starts with letter C. Look along this row to find the letter underneath the i at the top and you find it's **K**. Write it down before you forget it!

Now you move on to work out what code letter you need for the letter "l". The H above it tells you to use the row starting with letter H, and the letter on this row under the l is **S**. For the next letter you need the

row starting with I, and the letter under o which is
W. If you keep going with the other letters, you'll get:

keyword: C H I P S C H I P S C H I P S C H I P S C
plaintext: i l o v e v e r o n i c a g u m f l o s s
CODETEXT:K S W K W X L Z D F K J I V M O M T D K U

This code is now becoming extremely difficult to
break! It gets even tougher if you use a longer key, so
instead of CHIPS, you might use PONGO
MCWHIFFYS DELUXE BURGER BAR. If your key
is longer than the message, then the sequence of
rows you use will not repeat and it makes things even
tougher for the crackers. If only Mary Queen of Scots
had thought of using PONGO MCWHIFFYS
DELUXE BURGER BAR to mix up her messages, she
might still be alive today.

Breaking Blaise's code
You'd think that the changing code system invented
by Blaise de Vigenere was impossible to crack, but
some people simply have no respect for the word
"impossible" and one of them was Charles Babbage.
He was born in 1791 in London and invented all

sorts of odd things including a fantastic mechanical computer with 25,000 moving parts.

THIS IS THE LAPTOP VERSION!

It was in the 1850s that a dentist called John Thwaites teased him by saying that Blaise's code was uncrackable, so Babbage had a go. Don't forget that to break codes, you have to have a LOT of free time and you also need to be slightly mad. Here's roughly how Babbage did it.

To start with you need to be cracking a message that has hundreds of words, and you desperately hope that the keyword is only a few letters long. The first thing to do is to try and work out how many letters are in the keyword. You do this by looking for repeated groups of letters and seeing how far apart they are. This is a section of a longer message:

QOOHMF DNJICE SCRVTB GRQOOV ECENJI NAHKJQ OOPIWD CV

Look carefully and you'll spot the letters QOO appear three times. If you're dead lucky, then this means the same three-letter word has been repeated in the message. (Or it could be any group of three letters that often appear together such as "ing," "ere," or "ght.") It also means that the word has just happened to fall under the same letters of the keyword.

What you do is see how many letters are between the starts of the three QOOs. To make it easy to count, we'll write the message out with the digits 1-0 underneath and move the spaces:

```
CODETEXT:QOO  HMFDN J  I C E S C R V T B G R
letter count:  1 2 3   4 5 6 7 8 9 0 1 2 3 4 5 6 7 8 9 0
     QOO   VECEN J I NAHK J   QOO   P I WDCV
     1 2 3   4 5 6 7 8 9 0 1 2 3 4 5   6 7 8   9 0 1 2 3 4
```

Excitement!

After QOO first appears, it reappears exactly 20 letters later, and then 15 letters later it appears again. As the numbers 20 and 15 both divide by 5, this suggests that the keyword is five letters long. Now we'll write the message out again, but this time we'll divide it up into five-letter blocks and we'll put the numbers 1 2 3 4 5 above it to represent the five letters in the keyword.

keyword: 1 2 3 4 5   1 2 3 4 5   1 2 3 4 5
CODETEXT: QOOHM FDNJI   CESCR
1 2 3 4 5   1 2 3 4 5   1 2 3 4 5   1 2 3 4 5   1 2 3 4 5
VTBGR QOOVE CENJI NAHKJ QOOPI
1 2 3 4
WDCV

You'll see that QOO always appears under the numbers 123, and we've been really lucky here, because you'll notice the letters NJI appear twice, and both times they are under letters 3, 4, and 5 of the keyword. This makes us feel even more confident that the keyword is five letters long.

At this point, you have to try guessing what three letter combination QOO stands for. Eeek—what a horrible boring job! But luckily the mad old bloke who writes these books already knows the answer and as you are being lovely enough to read this, you're allowed to know that you should guess QOO = you.

Let's see how the keyword, the CODETEXT, and the guess all line up:

```
keyword:      1 2 3 4 5
CODETEXT:     Q O O H M
guess:          y o u
```

This tells us that the first letter of the keyword turns *y* into Q, so we should be able to work out what the key letter is. Look at the table and go down the *y* column until you reach Q. You'll find yourself on row 18, with the key letter S, so the first letter of the keyword is S. The second letter of the keyword turns *o* into O, so if you check the table you'll find the key letter = A. The third letter of the keyword turns out to be U.

So far we have S A U ? ? as the keyword, but it all depends on guessing that QOO = you.

```
keyword:      S A U 4 5
CODETEXT:     Q O O H M
guess:          y o u
```

THAT'S A LOT OF WORK JUST TO GET THREE LETTERS OF THE KEY WORD!

AND THEY MIGHT STILL BE WRONG. SO FAR WE'VE ONLY BEEN GUESSING!

There are two things you might try here.

- Remember that we have a repeated three letter arrangement NJI that was coded using letters 3, 4, and 5. Therefore the letter N was coded with the third letter of the keyword, which we think might be U. This means we can decode letter N using key letter U and we get letter *t*. It's time to take another guess—could the letters NJI be the three letter word "the"? (The mad old bloke who writes these books is nodding wisely.) Try working J = *h* and I = *e* backwards to see what they give you for the fourth and fifth key letters.

- The other thing to try is to have an instinctive guess at the keyword. Of course it might be some rubbish such as SAUQF or SAUJZ, but maybe it's a proper five-letter word? If so, do we have any clues as to what it might be? So far in this chapter we've had CHIPS as a keyword, so what might go with it? Um.. . .

68

And indeed, if you try SAUCE, you'll find the message will decode (although as it's a test message devised to show how to crack codes, it's not very interesting!).

Uncrackable code

Using this system it is possible to have a code that cannot be broken! Charles Babbage's method of breaking Blaise de Vigenere's code relied on a short keyword being repeated. If you use a key that is longer than the message then it won't repeat, and any patterns that arise in the letters will be purely accidental. A key can be anything from one word to a whole book. The only clues a cracker will ever get is if you send a message with a mistake and then send it again corrected, or if you send lots of messages using the same key. But if you always send messages using a different key every time that never repeats, you're safe.

So how do you get a key that always changes? Read on. . .

69

ONE-TIME PADS

One of the most classic ways to send an unbreakable code is to use code books and a "one-time pad." First we'll see what the code book does and then we'll see how the one-time pad comes into it.

The code book can be quite a chunky thing and there can be lots of copies of it. Generally a code book has hundreds of words in it along with all the individual letters A-Z. Everything is represented by five-digit numbers. Obviously you shouldn't be sending the crackers a copy as a birthday present, but if they do get hold of one, it doesn't really matter. It wouldn't even matter if the Gollarks from planet Zog got a copy.

If you wanted to send a message "a aardvark accidentally abolished a abbey," you could just swap all the words into numbers and get

38545 28367 11990 78645 38545 98653

The trouble is that if you did accidentally send the crackers a code book as a birthday present, they could easily work out what you had written.

However, now you've got the message written as numbers, you can encode this very securely using a one-time pad.

One-time pads tend to be very small to make them easy to hide, and there are only two copies made of each one. Your agent has one and you have the other. The pages of the pad aren't much bigger than a postage stamp and are full of random lists of numbers or letters. If a one-time pad is to work with a code book, it will be full of five-digit numbers like this:

Here's how to encode your message:

- Write the plaintext message out.
- Look up the code numbers in the code book and write them underneath.
- Underneath the row of code numbers, you copy out a set of numbers from the pad. (You and your agent have already decided which page of the pad you're going to be using for that message.)

● After you've used the page of your pad, you eat it.

WHERE DID THAT PAGE GO?

BURP... PARDON ME.

Oi! YOU'RE SUPPOSED TO EAT IT AFTER WE USE IT!

● Add the digits of the numbers using *clock adding*!

CLOCK ADDING

Clock adding is just like normal adding only you don't carry tens over.

Here's a dial with the numbers 0-9 around it.

If a hand points at 8 and then moves round four places, it ends up on 2.

So for clock adding 8 + 4 = 2.

- The finished row of numbers is your CODETEXT. Here's how our message might look as it's coded:

plaintext:	a	aardvark	accidentally
code nos:	38545	28367	11990
pad nos:	93267	07837	23462
CODETEXT:	21702	25194	34352

	abolished	a	abbey
	78645	38545	98653
	31980	66362	23167
	09525	94807	11710

When you're clock adding the digits of code, you work along doing the sums one at a time. Here the first sum is $3 + 9 = 2$. The next is $8 + 3 = 1$ then $5 + 2 = 7$ and so on. When you get used to it, it's very quick!

To decode, your agent simply goes along and subtracts the numbers you've used and then eats the page of the one-time pad. As long as the crackers don't have a copy of your one-time pad then your message is completely safe!

One-time pads and Blaise's table

If you don't have a code book, you can write out a message in plaintext. Underneath you write out a list of numbers from a one-time pad. (Obviously your agent must know which numbers you've used.) You then encode the message using different lines from Blaise de Vigenere's table. Below you'll see the number under the first "d" is 6 so we use line 6 of the table to turn "d" into J. (The 0 digit represents row 10.)

plaintext:	d o n t e	a t g r e	e n f i s	h
pad nos:	6 8 3 0 1	2 7 8 3 9	0 2 2 4 7	8
CODETEXT:	J W Q D F	C A O U N	O P H M Z	P

One-time pads can also contain sets of letters, and so you could use them as the key to encode your message. Because the pad provides you with a key that never repeats and never gets used again, any message sent with it is 100 percent secure.

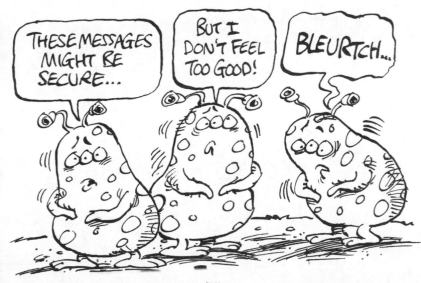

The Vernam cipher

One-time pads were a development of an idea that came from an American engineer called Gilbert Vernam in 1919 when people had just started sending messages by electricity. These days we use electricity to make all sorts of marvelous things possible such as embarrassing noises coming from your mobile phone when you're on the bus.

Back in Gilbert's time almost the only thing you could do with electricity was turn it on or off, but people still found ways of using it to send messages.

One very basic way to send a message with electricity would be to use our binary code and a light (see page 21). If you wanted to send the word "jelly," this translates into binary as

plaintext:	j	e	l	l	y
binary text:	10011	01110	10100	10100	11111

You send the message one digit at a time by giving your light a long flash for 1 and a short flash for 0.

Your agent can watch and write down a line of 1s and 0s, then when you've finished the agent can decode the binary text.

So far so good, but if anyone watching had read this book and knew your binary code, they could tell what the message said! So before you send your message, you encode it with a one-time pad.

Suppose your one-time pad started with the key letters ABCDE. You convert these into binary (with our binary code you get 01010, 01011, 01100, 01101, 01110) and then write the binary key underneath your binary text.

plaintext:	j	e	l	l	y
binary text:	10011	01110	10100	10100	11111
binary key:	01010	01011	01100	01101	01110

Here's the brilliant bit. You combine the binary text to the binary key using XOR.

XOR, NAND, and the good old days

If your head is starting to ache from numbers, CODETEXT, key letters, and so on, you'll be glad to know that we're now about to take a break from codes. XOR gives us an excuse to look at something that's simple and satisfying. We're going to see how computers got started and it doesn't involve any nasty programming or electronic knowledge, all you need to do is look at a few diagrams and follow a few lines.

In the old days when computers were just a pile of great big cog wheels and electromagnets, the very early calculations were all done using *logic gates*. The idea was that you had two inputs and one output.

It's a bit like having two switches and one light bulb. The switches can be set to 1 or 0 and the light can either be on or off.

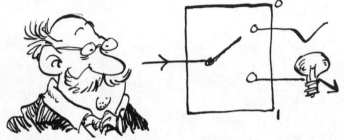

Here's a basic switch. The input is connected to the bit inside that moves up or down and so it can either connect to the 0 terminal or to the 1 terminal. We've wired a light bulb to the 1 terminal, so if the switch is in the 1 position then the light could come on, but try not to think of the switch as being on or off. If we had wired the bulb to the 0 terminal, it would come on if the switch was in the 0 position.

The fun starts when you combine two switches. Follow the wires in the diagrams to see the different things that can happen.

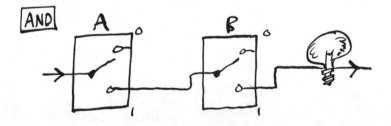

AND – the light will only go on if switch A = 1 AND switch B = 1.

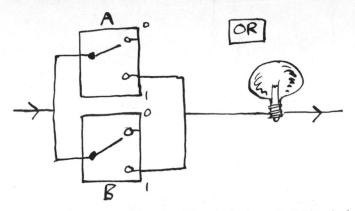

OR – the light will go on if switch A = 1 OR switch B = 1 (or both = 1).

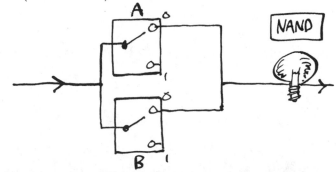

NAND – this means "not and" which is the opposite to AND. If A = 1 and B = 1, the light will be off. Otherwise it will be on!

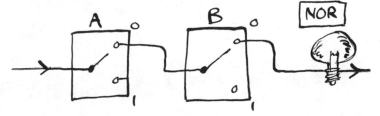

NOR – this is the opposite to OR. If A = 1 or B = 1 (or both = 1), then the light will be off.

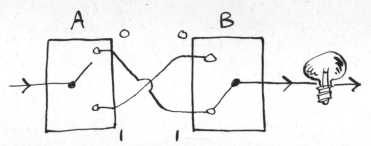

XOR – (short for "eXclusive OR") this is almost the same as OR because if A = 1 or B = 1, then the light is on. BUT . . . if they both = 1, or if they both = 0, the light will be off. In other words, if the switches are different, the light will be on, but if they are the same it will be off.

XOR is the logic for the Vernam code system that involves adding 1s and 0s.

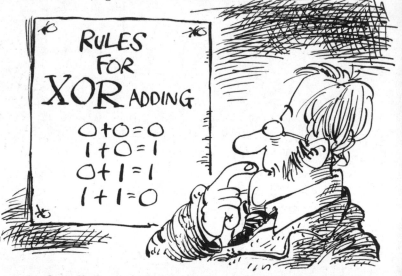

As for all these switches, you might think they are rather clumsy and outdated, but if you've got a mobile phone, the microchips inside it are jam packed full of them putting two things together and getting an answer. When trillions of these switches are working at once, they can produce music, pictures, connect to the Internet, and tell you the time. And they can even make embarrassing noises when you really don't need them.

Back to code

So where did we get to? Oh yes, we were about to add each digit of the binary text to the digits of the binary key using XOR:

```
plaintext:    j       e       l       l       y
binary text:  10011   01110   10100   10100   11111
binary key:   01010   01011   01100   01101   01110
CODETEXT:     11001   00101   11000   11001   10001
```

Now are you ready for the *really* cool bit? You send your CODETEXT and your agent writes it down. To decode it the agent ADDS the binary key again using XOR!

```
CODETEXT:     11001   00101   11000   11001   10001
binary key:   01010   01011   01100   01101   01110
binary text:  10011   01110   10100   10100   11111
```

This is the amazing thing about XOR. If you add the binary key twice, you get back to the original binary message. Then your agent just turns the binary message back into letters and *Wahey!* you're finished.

Of course it's unlikely you'll be using this sort of secret message, but when Gilbert invented this system, it showed the world how good computers were going to be at codes.

GRID CODES

City: **Chicago, Illinois, USA**
Place: **Luigi's Diner, Upper Main St**
Date: **12 November 1929**
Time: **11:30 am**

Luigi licked his top lip and looked nervously towards the six shady men sitting round the central table of his diner. The three Boccelli brothers had been joined by the Gabriannis and together they were all staring mournfully at a bowl in the middle of the table that contained the remains of a pile of squaralini pasta and no sauce. Squaralini is plain squares of pasta that nobody has bothered to make into a fancy shape. It looks ugly, it's dull to eat, and if you can afford to put sauce on it, it just slides off. In fact, there's only one reason why anyone would ever order squaralini pasta. It was cheap, dirt cheap.

"What's keeping him?" demanded the smallest man at the table, his head hardly visible under his hat. Behind Luigi's counter a green curtain hung across a doorway leading to a back room. The small man turned to check it, but there was no sign of movement.

"Come on, Half-Smile," he moaned. "We're all waiting."

"Cool it, Weasel," said Chainsaw Charlie, who was sitting beside him. "He'll be out in a minute."

The largest man at the table looked at the empty bowl and sighed. Then, without thinking, he picked up a fork and started to suck it.

"We're so broke, Porky's even eating the cutlery now," said the Weasel.

"Relax," said One Finger Jimmy. "Blade's plan is a peach. Tell 'em, Blade."

"It can't fail," said the man in the black suit. "These security uniforms that Jimmy picked up from Stitch Fuldrag, they're the real deal. All we do is put them on, wait by a bank, then when the shift changes over we march right in and then march right out again with the dough."

"So just as soon as we know which bank to hit, we'll be in business," said Jimmy.

"You mean you don't know which bank we're hitting?" blurted out Chainsaw in astonishment.

"Shhh!" said Blade, looking around nervously. But he needn't have bothered, there were no other customers in the place. "We don't want to hit an empty one. Dolly Snowlips is doing the rounds right now. She'll be along any time to tell us which one holds the jackpot."

"Whichever bank it is, if the uniforms aren't perfect, they'll be on to us immediately," said the Weasel.

"Stitch worked in the movies," said Blade. "And when you work in movies, every detail has to be perfect, even in close-up. You'll see when Half-Smile comes out."

As Blade spoke the green curtain twitched aside and Benni the waiter appeared.

"Mr Gabrianni's ready," said Benni. "It looks really good."

"Then bring him out," said Blade.

"Yeah!" laughed Charlie. "We want the fashion show."

Benni pulled the curtain aside and Half-Smile Gabrianni's face peered through. As ever the face had half a smile and half a scowl, but if it came to an umpire's decision, the scowl was definitely winning. He took a deep breath and stepped forward to stand behind the counter. Blade became aware of a strange noise in the restaurant, and to his surprise he realized it was the sound of the others clapping.

"It's good!" exclaimed the Weasel.

"Nice blue jacket," said Chainsaw Charlie. "Nice blue hat, too."

"And a nice clean shirt!" remarked One-Finger Jimmy. "I never saw him in a clean shirt before."

"Hey, Half-Smile, you better watch yourself," grinned the Weasel. "You'll ruin our family's reputation. It almost looks like you're going straight!"

TINK

Half-Smile scowled even more. It wasn't a pretty sight. In fact, it was so awful that there was a little *tink* noise as Porky accidentally bit the end off the fork. Blade tried to lighten the mood.

"So who put that tidy knot in your tie?" he asked.

"Oh that was me," said Benni. "She was having trouble so I gave her a hand."

A silence fell as everyone checked Half-Smile's security outfit again. Would it pass even the closest close-up? Surely it looked perfect, but then. . .

"*She?*" exclaimed the Weasel. "What do you mean *she* was having trouble, so you gave *her* a hand?"

"Ah. . ." said Benny uncertainly. It was only a very quiet "ah" but it was enough for Luigi. His diner had been wrecked so many times that he could spot trouble coming a mile away, even if it was dressed up in a security uniform with a matching hat. Luigi dived into the fridge and slammed the door shut behind him. Half-Smile stepped out from behind the counter. Everybody gasped.

"If I step outside wearing this, I'll be going straight all right," growled Half Smile. "Straight into the women's prison."

Suddenly the uniform didn't look so good in close up. Half-Smile's hairy knees were sticking out from under the hem of the blue uniform skirt.

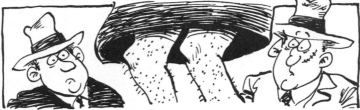

"You clowns!" shrieked the Weasel at Blade. "Your buddy sent skirts instead of pants. Are you Boccellis trying to make us all look stupid?"

Chairs shot backwards from the table as the six men leapt to their feet. Five of them were pointing guns accusingly at each other, and one was pointing a fork handle.

"No, please!" came a muffled voice from inside the fridge. "Don't smash the place up again."

"Let's all take a slow breath, guys," said Blade. "It's just a tiny hitch."

"It's still a good plan," insisted Jimmy. "There's time for me to get down to Stitch's place and grab seven pairs of security pants, then get back here."

"Then make it fast," said Chainsaw. "Because I hate wearing skirts. I haven't worn a skirt since. . ."

"Since when?" asked Jimmy.

"Don't change the subject," said Chainsaw, whipping a penknife-size chain saw out of his pocket. "Like I said, make it FAST!"

Chainsaw tugged a tiny string and the chain saw

started up with nasty *vezzz* noise right next to Jimmy's nose, so Jimmy made it fast. He dived out of

VEZZZ

the front door and hurried away down Upper Main St towards West and 19th, just as a dainty clicking noise was approaching from South and 23rd.

"That's Dolly's footsteps!" said Blade. "Act natural or she'll refuse to cooperate." Immediately they all sat down and tried to look intelligent.

A red hat, coat, skirt and shoes, and lipstick stepped into the diner. Dolly Snowlips looked around but didn't sit down.

"Glad to see everything's looking normal in here for once," she said.

"Thank you, Miss Snowlips," said the fridge.

THANK YOU...

"You got everything sorted, Blade?" said Dolly. "'Cos I don't work with fools."

"Everything's peachy," said Blade trying to do a reassuring nod. Dolly was looking at Half-Smile who was sitting at the table with the edge of the tablecloth pulled up to his stomach. "What do you think of the uniform?"

"Is that what it is?" asked Dolly. "Then let's see it. Up you get, handsome."

Without thinking, Half-Smile stood up.

"PSSST!" hissed all the men, and together they winked and pointed at his skirt. Half-Smile immediately dashed round behind the counter and tried to stand there looking casual. Had Dolly noticed? Half-Smile was half blushing, but luckily Dolly wasn't showing any surprise.

"It looks good," admitted Dolly. She sounded impressed. "Although maybe the hat should be a little further forward."

"Further forward," repeated Half-Smile, adjusting the hat. "Gottit."

"And the tie, just a little to the left," said Dolly.

"Tie to the left," said Half-Smile, adjusting it.

"So have you got us a bank?" asked Blade.

Dolly gave Half-Smile a final approving glance. "Sure, I've got you a bank," she said. "But you better get moving. They've got a big payroll arriving in about an hour, so be down there and ready. It's Goldtopps."

"Goldtopps!" they all grinned.

"Goldtopps," repeated Dolly and she turned to go. Half-Smile breathed a sigh of relief. It was just as Dolly was stepping outside that she looked back and said, "Oh, just one more thing. Lower the hem slightly."

"Eh?"

Dolly indicated her own skirt which reached down to finish neatly at the top of her calves.

"Showing your knees is just *so* last year."

Dolly was gone and everyone got ready to leave too.

"We don't have long," said Blade. "We better get down there and be changed all ready."

"But we haven't got pants!" said Porky.

"As soon as Jimmy joins us with the pants, we pull them on and get in there," said Blade.

"But how will Jimmy know where we are?"

"We'll leave a message with Luigi," said Blade.

"Oh no!" wailed the fridge. "No message. It's Tuesday, we do meatballs and Lieutenant Ptchowsky always comes in. If he asks me anything I don't want to know. He could shut me down. And then where else would you get squaralini pasta?"

"We could write it on a slip of paper," said Porky. "Maybe stick it on the fridge."

"No!" said the fridge. "I don't want to be arrested."

"Surely the Lieutenant wouldn't arrest a fridge?" said Benni.

"He would," said everyone and the fridge.

But Blade was staring at a hole in the old table-cloth near the upper left corner. Through it he could see a letter G. He was thinking.

"Say, Benni, what's with this table?"

Blade pulled the cloth away, and written all over the surface of the table underneath were rows of letters.

"It came from the school," explained Benni. "All the kids, they write their initials on it. See, there's my B for Benni. After so many years, it got full up."

"There's an O, and there's an L . . ." murmured Blade. "I've got it! Chainsaw, lend me that little vezzy thing of yours."

Blade carefully laid the cloth back over the table so that the letter G appeared in the hole again. Using the mini chain saw, he cut several more little squares out of the tablecloth.

"Hey!" said Benni. "What you doing?"

"Relax," said Blade. "Once we're back from the bank I'll buy you a new tablecloth and a new table to go with it!"

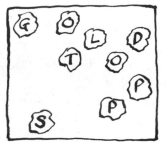

Soon there were nine little holes all over the cloth, and through each hole was a letter. The letters spelt G O L D T O P P S. Blade whisked away the cloth.

"Now listen up, Benni," said Blade. "When Jimmy comes back, he needs to know where we've gone. All you do is put the cloth back on the table and tell him to look at the letters. Got that?"

Benni nodded. He got it.

Grid Codes

A special way of hiding messages is to use a grid of letters or words and a "mask." The mask is a bit of paper with holes cut out that you put over the grid, then when you look through the holes you can see the letters or words you need. If you and your agent both have copies of the same book, you can make a mask that you put over a certain page and so reveal the message.

With books, you are a bit limited because you can only use the words and letters on the page, so it's often better (and more fun) to make your own letter grids to send messages.

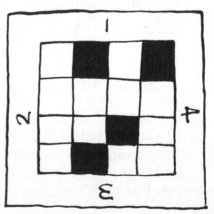

Here's a square grid of 16 letters that make up a complete message. You can't read it, can you? No? Good, because it's the most secret and dangerous message in this whole book. Next to the grid is the mask that goes over it and the clever part is that when you put the mask on the grid, you can have number 1, 2, 3, or 4 at the top. Each position will reveal four different letters.

We daren't print what the message says, but we'll give you a clue. Earlier on, we saw that Dolly Snowlips described her size as NYM, but there's some more detailed information here. Ooooh! Here's how to read the message if you dare.

- Copy out the mask and cut out the four holes (or if you're clever, you can just imagine it).
- Put it over the grid with 1 on top and write down the letters you see in order starting on the top line, then the next line and so on.

- Rotate the grid so that 2 is on top and write down the letters.
- Repeat with 3 and then 4 on top.
- Finally you have the message, but whatever you do . . . *don't tell Dolly you know!*

Unfortunately when Blade Boccelli was leaving the message for Jimmy in the diner, he didn't realize that grids could be rotated.

City: Chicago, Illinois, USA
Place: Luigi's Diner, Upper Main St
Date: 12 November 1929
Time: 11:50 am

It was about twenty minutes after Blade and the others had left that Jimmy arrived back at the diner clutching a parcel of pants. At first, he didn't see anyone so he went over to speak to the fridge.

"Say, where did everyone go?" he asked.

"Now there's a suspicious thing," said a voice from behind him. "One-Finger Jimmy talking to a fridge. I got to ask myself why would he be doing that?"

Jimmy turned round to see an unwelcome face in a side booth.

"Lieutenant Ptchowsky!" he gasped. "I was just looking for Luigi."

Luigi arrived behind the counter with an icicle hanging from his nose and carrying a plate of meatballs.

"You got a message for me?" asked Jimmy.

"N . . . n . . . no!" said Luigi with a shiver.

"You sure?"

"Answer the man!" drawled Ptchowsky.

"No message," said Luigi. "But perhaps you'd like to sit down and Benni will lay the table for you."

Luigi indicated the central table that had a perfect white tablecloth on it, then hurried over to deliver the meatballs to the lieutenant. Benni appeared out of the kitchen clutching another cloth as a bewildered Jimmy took his seat.

"Let me give you a nice new tablecloth," insisted Benni.

"I ain't got time for the niceties of gastronomic etiquette!" hissed Jimmy. "Besides, this cloth's new!"

"Er . . . but this one is even newer!" said Benni opening the old cloth with the holes cut in it.

"What's going on there?" the lieutenant asked Luigi. "That ain't no new cloth."

"He's a . . . a very messy customer," whispered Luigi. "We keep the best cloths for our special customers such as you, sir."

The lieutenant grunted his approval then started to attack the meatballs as if they'd just been brought in for questioning. Meanwhile, Benni had set the old cloth out on the central table.

"Look at the holes in this cloth!" muttered Jimmy.

"No sir, *you* look at them," insisted Benni.

"Me?" demanded Jimmy. "Why should I. . ."

But then he looked, and as he did so a big smile

crept across his face. "Well I'll be blessed!" And he dashed out of the door and hurried away down the street.

Benni went to scoop up the tablecloth, but just as he was about to whisk it away, something caught his eye.

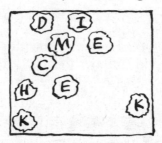

"Dimechekk?" said Benni. "Oh no, how did that happen?"

Make your own masks and grids

It's good fun designing a grid message with a rotating mask because it uses a special bit of math that doesn't involve sums.

First of all, you need to decide how big your grid is and this relies on how many letters you need for your message. This table shows the size of grid, the number of letters, and the number of holes in the mask.

Letters	Size	Holes
16	4 × 4	4
24	5 × 5	6
36	6 × 6	9
48	7 × 7	12
64	8 × 8	16
80	9 × 9	20

We're going to see how to design a 5 × 5 grid, and to make it clear what's going on, we'll just use a very simple test message: A B C D E F G H I J K L M N O P Q R S T U V W X.

Get two square bits of paper and draw a 5 × 5 grid of squares on both of them. One piece of grid will have the letters on it and the other will become the mask.

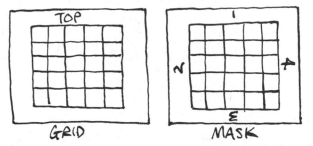

Next, you have to decide on where the holes go in your mask. You have to make sure that when you rotate it, the same letter doesn't appear twice. Set the mask in position 1 (i.e. number 1 is on top). *If your grid has an ODD number of squares, you can't use the very middle square, so we'll mark it with a + to remind us.* Now we'll put a hole in any square we like and see what happens:

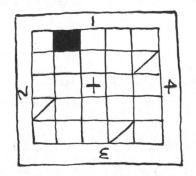

We've marked the hole in black and we've put it on the top line. We've also marked in / stripes to show where the hole will appear when the mask is rotated. These stripes tell us that we can't put holes in any of these squares. We now put a second hole in any of the other unmarked squares.

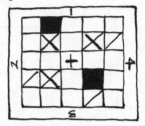

You'll see we've put X in the places this second hole will appear when the mask is rotated. You can now choose any of the other unmarked squares for the next hole and mark the places the hole will appear when the grid rotates. You then put in your next hole and repeat the process, and keep putting holes in until all the squares either have holes or marks. In a 5 × 5 grid, you'll end up with six holes. The mask is finished!

Now you put your mask on top of the second grid and then you can write in the first letters of your message.

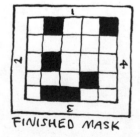

FINISHED MASK

PUT MASK ON TOP OF GRID. WRITE LETTERS IN THE HOLES.

Here are the six holes and the letters ABCDEF are written in. Next you rotate the mask to position 2 and write in the next six letters, then do the same for position 3. When you turn the mask to position 4, it's really satisfying that the last blank spaces finish exactly under the holes!

Here's how our test message will appear with the mask removed:

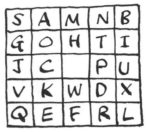

S	A	M	N	B
G	O	H	T	I
J	C		P	U
V	K	W	D	X
Q	E	F	R	L

City: Chicago, Illinois, USA
Place: Goldtopps Alley
Date: 12 November 1929
Time: 12:29 pm

Down a dark alley at the side of Goldtopps Bank was parked a Dodge Sedan with the windows steamed up. Inside sat six shady men, all wearing nice clean shirts, blue peaked hats, jackets, and ties.

"Everyone ready?" asked Blade. They all nodded. They were all ready, or at least they were as ready as they could be without any trousers on.

"As soon as Jimmy gets here, we pull those pants on and go to work," said Blade.

"What's keeping him?" asked the Weasel, trying to peer through the misted-up glass.

"Shhh!" said Blade. "Listen, this could be him now!"

Footsteps approached and there was a tap on the window. Blade wound it down a fraction.

"Hey, boys!" said Dolly Snowlips.

Immediately they all took their hats off and held them over their laps.

"You guys going to do this or not?" asked Dolly crossly. "Another ten minutes and that payroll will be all packed into little envelopes and sent out."

"But . . . but we can't move right now!" said Blade.

"You're going to have to," said Dolly, "because you're parked in a red zone. They've come to tow the car away."

"WHAT?" they all gasped. They wound the windows down and sure enough, they saw a huge tow truck backing towards them with a big hook swinging from the back. Dolly took a step backwards as the hook clanged into the car and seconds later the front of the vehicle was rising into the air.

"Arghhh!" came six voices.

The car doors burst open, the six men piled out and made a dash for it, out of the alley and past the entrance to the bank. Soon there was a loud roar of laughter as all the bank employees rushed out to see the flapping shirt tails and twelve hairy legs hurrying away down the streets. There were whistles, jeers, cat calls, and there was also the quiet clicking noise of a pair of red shoes stepping down the deserted corridors of the bank towards the secure vault, which had been left open.

Later that night the seven shady men were all back at Luigi's. But before they had time to order one bowl of squaralini with seven forks, Benni wheeled out a trolley loaded with lobster, ravioli, steaks, sauces, and pineapple chunks on dainty little sticks.

"Eat up, boys!" announced Luigi from behind his counter. "It's all been paid for. Somebody you know just came into a whole load of money and wants to say thanks."

"Thanks for what?"

"There was some message about you guys distracting all the bank staff, and so when they weren't looking. . ." Luigi stopped suddenly and glanced at the side booth. Thankfully the lieutenant had left hours ago. "Anyway, I don't do messages, so that's all. Now eat up."

They just sat there dumbfounded.

"I don't get it," said the Weasel. "Who would treat us to dinner?"

"Hold on!" grinned Benni. Once again he unfolded the old cloth and held it up ready to lay across the table.

THE ANSWER'S IN THE HOLES!

"But it says GOLDTOPPS," said Blade.

"Goldtopps?" gasped Jimmy. "When I read it, it said DIMECHEKK. That's why I took the pants to Dimechekk bank. I felt pretty foolish, I can tell you."

"GRRRR," growled all the others.

"YOU felt foolish?" said Half-Smile. "What about us?"

"You were OK," said Porky. "You could have worn your skirt."

It was getting nasty again, but Benni had already laid out the cloth and was pouring out the Vino Pronto.

"Come on, it's all forgotten, guys," said Blade. "Forget the message. Let's just raise a glass to whoever paid for this, although we might never know."

The seven men all stood and clinked their glasses. "To whoever it is, although we might never know," they cheered.

THE ENIGMA MACHINE

During the First World War, a German inventor called Arthur Scherbius decided that the codes and ciphers being used weren't up to much, and so he sat down and invented the best code machine the world has ever known. In 1918, he filed the first patent on his Enigma machine and over the following years he kept improving it. By the end of the Second World War, the German army had bought 30,000 of them and in many ways it was a far more useful weapon than tanks or bombs.

The Enigma machine was about the same size and weight of five laptops piled on top of each other. When you opened the top, here's what you saw:

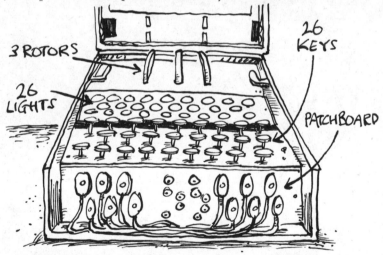

- A sort of old-fashioned typewriter keyboard with 26 clunky buttons labeled with the letters of the alphabet.
- A display of 26 letters that could each light up.

- There was also what looked like the three reels of a fruit machine, but instead of pictures of cherries and melons, these reels (or *rotors* as they should be called) had letters on. You could pull the rotors out and swap them round.
- At the front of the machine was a *patch board* that looked like rows of headphone sockets labeled A–Z. You could connect pairs of these holes together with special wires called *patch cords*.
- Some extra buttons and dials to make it look more exciting.

The Enigma machine encodes messages using a similar system to Blaise de Vigenere's table of letters. The clever bit is that rather than using a few keywords that keep repeating themselves, Enigma behaves as if it has a key that runs into thousands of letters before it repeats.

How to work the Enigma machine

First of all you take the three rotors out and swap them round, then put them back in. You make a note of what order you put them in, and also what letter is showing at the top of each rotor. (Your agent would need to know all this to decode the message.) You might also plug up to six patch cords across the holes at the front of the machine to connect pairs of letters up. Your agent would need to know which letters were connected too. So for instance you might tell your agent the rotors were in the order 3–1–2, the starting positions were *gvq*, and the patch cords were connected as follows: P–Y, G–R, N–F, D–S, C–X, U–K. All this information makes up the key to your message.

Now all you do is type in your plaintext message, one letter at a time. Each time you push a key, a different letter on the display would light up and you would copy it down.

To decode a message, your agent uses the key to set up his Enigma machine in exactly the same way as you did with the reels and six patch cords in the right place. Then he types in the coded message and the plaintext message would be spelt out by the lights!

How does it work?

The Enigma machine used electrical contacts to connect the keys and the lights, and the contacts changed for every letter you typed in. Get ready for some bad news and then some good news.

Bad news: it's a bit tricky explaining how the original electric Enigma machine works.

Good news: we're going to MAKE one! All we need is some paper, a pencil, and a pair of scissors. Even though our version won't be electric, it works in almost exactly the same way as the electric machine. Even if you don't actually make it, if you follow the instructions you'll see how it works.

How to make the Murderous Maths Enigma machine

To keep things simple, we're just going to make a version that encodes and decodes the first eight letters of the alphabet. Once you've understood it, if you're keen you can go on to make a proper 26-letter version.

You need four circles of paper of different sizes. (When you put them together, they will look like the picture on page 109.)

We'll number them 1–4 with the smallest being disc 1 and the biggest being disc 4. Pile them together in order with their centers aligned. Draw around the edge of disc 1 so that a circle appears on disc 2. Now draw around the edge of disc 2 to put a circle on disc 3 and finally draw around disc 3 to put a circle on disc 4.

- Take disc 1 and divide it up into eight sectors. Label these ABCDEFGH.
- Take disc 2 and put eight marks evenly spaced around the circle you drew on it. Put an "X" next

DISC 1.

to one of these marks. Now put eight marks around the edge in line with the other marks. Here comes the fun bit—draw a line to link each mark on the circle to *any* one of the marks on the edge of the disc. When you've finished, each of the inner marks should be linked to a different mark on the edge. The lines can cross over but be sure to make them clear and the best way of doing that is if you make each line a different colour. Even though your Murderous Maths Enigma machine might be regarded as a devastating weapon of war, at least it will be a pretty one.

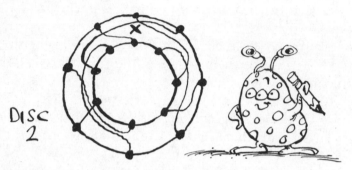

DISC 2

- Take disc 3 and do exactly the same as you did for disc 2 but your links should be in a different pattern.
- With disc 4, only put 8 marks around the circle, and mark one with an X. You then draw lines to link the eight marks up in pairs. Again the lines can cross over but do make them clear.

DISC 4

- Now put your four discs together and pin them in the center so that you can turn them round independently. Incidentally, we should have told you to make your discs a convenient size, not twice as big as yourself.

- Finally make an exact copy of everything you've done and give it to your agent. Otherwise you'll be encoding fabulously difficult messages and nobody will be able to read them, which is a bit sad. You should end up with something like this:

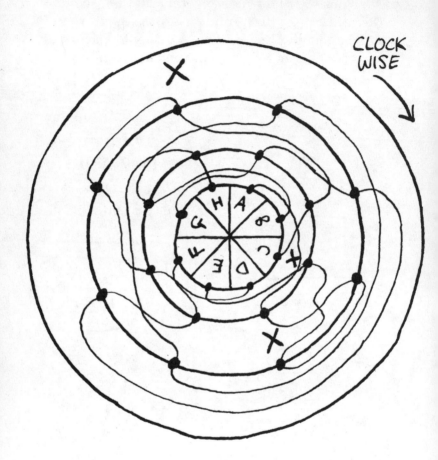

You'll notice that we've got the X on disc 2 lined up with letter C on disc 1. The X on disc 3 is lined up with letter D and the X on disc 4 is lined up with letter H. These letters CDH are the starting position of the discs. Of course you can choose any starting position you like, so long as you let your agent know what it is!

How to encode a message

We'll encode "aaa" and see what happens.

- Follow the line that leads from the letter A on disc 1. It goes across disc 2, then disc 3, then disc 4, then back over disc 3, then disc 2, and ends up at **E**.
- Now you turn disc 1 one place clockwise!

DISC 1 IS THE SMALL ONE IN THE MIDDLE.

- Letter A is now where letter B was, so to encode "a" follow the line from letter A out to disc 4 and back to find that it ends up at **G**. (If you're looking at the picture, remember disc 1 has rotated one place, so G has moved to where H is on the picture.)
- Turn disc 1 one place clockwise again!
- Letter A is now where letter C was. Follow the line out to disc 4 and back to find that it ends up at **B**. (Don't forget the disc has rotated again.)

So far our message "aaa" has become EGB.

If you have a really long plaintext message, you would keep turning disc 1 one place for every new letter. However, after you had encoded eight letters, A will be back at the starting place. When this happens you turn disc 2 one place clockwise. You then encode eight more letters, turning disc 1 one place every time. When A gets round to the starting place, you turn disc 2 one more place and continue.

After you've encoded 64 letters, you'll find both discs 1 and 2 are back where they started. So you turn disc 3 one place clockwise . . . and on you go!

111

Using this little machine, if you were encoding a long line of "aaaaaaa . . ." you'd get a mixed-up pattern of letters that would not repeat until 512 letters had passed!

To decode your message, your agent just has to set the wheels on his Enigma machine to the same starting position as yours. The first message of the CODETEXT is **E**, so when he follows the line it will come out at "a." He then turns disc 1 one place clockwise, and he'll find the the second letter of the code G comes out as "a" and so on.

Our machine is fine for messages that just need the letters A–H, such as this ultimate Gollark insult:

If you need a machine to encode all 26 letters, then you can make a bigger version with 26 letters around disc 1. Discs 2, 3, and 4 have 26 marks around the circles that are all joined up in the same way as before.

How the real Enigma machine works
The real machine had three "rotors" in it.

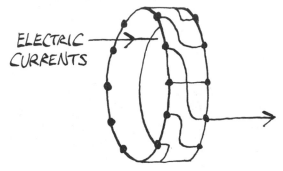

Each rotor had 26 electrical points on each side, and they were connected up in pairs in a completely mixed-up fashion, just like discs 2 and 3 on our MM Enigma machine. Each rotor could turn around, meaning it kept changing the pathway of connections inside the machine.

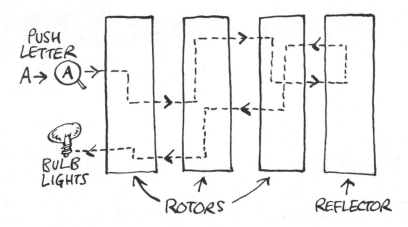

Each of the 26 keys on the keyboard was connected to one of the points on the side of the first rotor. When a letter key was pushed, an electric current passed through the rotor to a point on the other side. The other side of the first rotor was connected to the second rotor, and this was connected to the third rotor. After the third rotor was a "reflector," which had 26 points connected in pairs like our disc 4. This sent the current back through the three rotors and when it finally came out again it was wired to one of the 26 letter bulbs. Every time a letter key was pushed, at least one of the rotors changed its connections and that's how the messages were encoded.

As there were three rotors with 26 connections on each, this meant the number of possible starting positions for the rotors was $26 \times 26 \times 26 = 17,576$. (This also means that if you kept typing "aaaa . . ." you'd get 17,576 letters before the pattern repeated!) You could also swap the three rotors round into a different order, and there are $3 \times 2 \times 1 = 6$ ways of doing that. This gave you a total of $17,576 \times 6 = 105,456$ possible starting positions.

As if that wasn't clever enough . . .

Arthur Scherbius had built a machine that happily mangled the alphabet to bits, but he didn't like the idea of the alphabet being in the usual order in the first place.

With our own little MM Enigma machine, you can't swap the "rotors" round but you can make life more complicated for crackers by changing the letters round on disc 1.

114

With the real Enigma machine, you plugged the six patch cords into the sockets at the front to swap round pairs of letters on the keyboard. If you connected M to Z then when you pushed letter M, you got a coding for letter Z.

Just in case you're interested, there are 100,391,791,500 different ways of connecting the six patch cords between the 26 holes. If you've read The Perfect Sausage and Other Fundamental Formulas, *you'll be desperate to know that the formula to work this out comes from mixing up the "alien interpreters" formula that uses triangle numbers, and the permutations formula. If h = number of holes and c = number of patch cords, the formula for the number of different ways you can link pairs of holes =*

$$\frac{h!}{(2^c \times c! \times (h - 2c)!)}$$

If the Enigma machine just had the patch cords but no rotors, it would be very similar to using a basic code strip with a keyword, and crackers would have just laughed at it. But when the alphabet was mixed up and *then* mangled, they weren't laughing.

ENIGMA WITHOUT ROTORS

ENIGMA WITH ROTORS

Was Enigma perfect?

The Enigma machine itself had one tiny weakness. Without using the patch cords if you encoded letter a, you would never get A. (Look at the MM Enigma machine—you'll see if you follow a line from one letter across the discs and back, it always has to come back to a different letter.) This meant that if crackers were desperately testing out lots of meanings for a piece of code, it eliminated some of the possibilities.

What really spoilt it for Enigma though was that the French had a spy who got photographs of the plans and passed them on to the Polish code breakers. The Germans weren't silly, they had always imagined that at some point the details of the machine would leak out—after all there were 30,000 of the things. So what the Germans did was develop a clever *day-key* system so that their Enigma machines were set up differently at the start of each day. Even when other countries had built their own Enigma machines, before they could crack the codes they needed to know the three details of the day-key:

● The six patchcord settings (e.g. U–G, H–J, K–E, F–X, L–D, and C–Z)
● The order of the three rotors (e.g. 2–3–1)
● The starting positions of each rotor (e.g. *pnw*)

The Germans still weren't happy with this. If the crackers managed to break just one part of a message, then it would make all the thousands of messages sent that day much easier to crack. So to make things even trickier, the Germans changed the starting positions of the rotors for every message!

As this is getting confusing, here's a strange little

scene to demonstrate what was going on.

You and your agent can speak several billion different languages. You want a private chat but you know that an evil alien power is spying on you and you suspect that they have learnt to understand your language of the day: English.

Although you start your conversation in English, the first thing you say to your agent is the new language you're going to speak in. To make absolutely sure your agent gets the right language, you say it twice.

Then for the rest of your conversation you talk in a different language.

The Germans did the same thing with Enigma, but instead of choosing a different language, they chose different rotor settings. Here's what the signallers would do:

- They set up the Enigma with the day-key.
- They chose any three letters: e.g. *jsw*.
- They wrote these letters out twice to make sure there was no confusion: *jswjsw*.
- They encoded this into a six-letter message, for example HTYXCQ, and sent it.
- They reset the rotors in their Enigma machine to the new starting position (*jsw*). The patchcord settings and the order of the rotors stayed the same.
- They would continue with the rest of the message.
- If they sent another message, they would reset the rotors to the day-key position, choose three new letters, and start again. The message would then be coded completely differently.

Cracking Enigma
Breaking any good substitution code is the equivalent of doing a massive jigsaw puzzle, but without knowing what the picture is going to be.

But as the Enigma code keeps changing in patterns you don't know, it's like doing it in the dark.

Cracking Enigma might seem impossible, but about fifteen years after the first Enigma machine was built, the crackers started to beat it. Sorry, but this book is not going to explain how they did it. That's partly because it's screamingly complicated, but mainly it's because even if we could sort it out before we ran out of space, you would never appreciate the phenomenal brainpower and millions of working hours the crackers spent on it. If the crackers had just been a couple of bored people having a go instead of doing the newspaper crossword over a coffee, they would never have done it. In reality it took thousands of people, including mathematicians, language experts, and chess champions, who were desperate not to have their country invaded and all their families split up and sent to ghastly labor camps.

What we will do is give credit to two of the mental giants responsible.

Marian Rejewski was the Polish genius who lead the team that first cracked Enigma in the 1930s. They were based in a part of Poland that had been in Germany 20 years before, which was very useful because it meant that they could all speak German. Even though Marian was faced with millions of jumbled letters, he discovered a weakness in the repeated three-letter key that started each message. In terms of doing the massive jigsaw in the dark, the repeated key was the equivalent of finding the four-corner pieces.

After many long months of patience and frustration, the early Enigma messages started to be decoded. Although the Germans weren't told about the crackers' success, they got suspicious and added a couple of spare rotors with different wiring.

Marian managed to overcome the extra problems by building machines called "bombes" that analyzed thousands of possible combinations and possibilities to produce messages. By the time the Second World

War started in 1939, a top secret base had been set up in Bletchley Park in England for breaking Enigma codes. For 35 years, nobody knew about this base or the people who worked there, so while the rest of the world was using Enigma thinking it was uncrackable, Bletchley Park could read everything.

Our second mental giant was one of the secret crackers at Bletchley Park called Alan Turing.

Marian's way of cracking Enigma relied on the repeated message key, but the crackers had to be prepared for the day when people stopped repeating the key.

Millions of messages and their meanings had been stored away over the years, and Alan Turing decided it was worth checking the plaintexts for patterns to try and predict when words like "weather" "arrival" and "confirm" would appear. (These would be in

German or other languages of course!) By doing that, he gradually managed to undo small sections of code and finally crack complete messages.

AT LAST... FINISHED!

Don't ask how he did it, but it involved new "bombe" machines the size of delivery vans and a massive team of extremely clever people. It's fair to say his genius did a lot to help shorten the war, but he never got any public thanks for it because Bletchely Park was so secret. Everyone just thought Alan was a weed who had managed to skip being in the army. Despite being a lovely, friendly, and scruffy bloke, he died in terribly sad personal circumstances without even his family knowing what he did. That's why we've made a point of mentioning him here, because his brains and dedication make him a true Murderous Maths hero.

NUMBER MESSAGES

If you turn letters into numbers, this gives you a whole new range of ways to encode messages. The easiest way to turn letters into numbers is this:

a = 1	b = 2	c = 3	d = 4	e = 5
f = 6	g = 7	h = 8	i = 9	j = 10
k = 11	l = 12	m = 13	n = 14	o = 15
p = 16	q = 17	r = 18	s = 19	t = 20
u = 21	v = 22	w = 23	x = 24	y = 25
z = 26				

HINT: Here are a few letters that make remembering this list easier: **I** = n**I**ne, **L** = twe**L**ve, and **T** = **T**wen**T**y. Otherwise remember the word *ejot* because these are the 5th, 10th, 15th, and 20th letters.

Here's how "hello granny" would look:
8 5 12 12 15 7 18 1 14 14 25

OH, THAT'S NICE!

Encoding number messages

The fun comes when you encode your numbers with a few sums! By now you'll be able to think of your own ideas, but here are a couple to get you started.

● **Key numbers**

You and your agent decide on a number, such as 6235. You write the digits of the key number under the

124

numbers in the CODETEXT, then add them together. Here's how the finished coding would look:

plaintext:	h	e	l	l	o	g	r	a	n	n	y
code numbers:	8	5	12	12	15	7	18	1	14	14	25
key number:	6	2	3	5	6	2	3	5	6	2	3
CODETEXT:	14	7	15	17	21	9	21	6	20	16	28

OOH!

The nice thing about this system is that it gets rid of the double letters. (This code is used for the mystery tour in *Professor Fiendish's Book of Brain-benders*.)

● **Chains**

Write out your message, but add a key letter at the front. Next, turn the message into numbers. Finally, add each number to the next one and write the answer underneath. That's the CODETEXT! Here we've used key letter q.

KEY LETTER

PLAIN TEXT	q	h	e	l	l	o	g	r	a	n	n	y
CODE NUMBERS	17	8	5	12	12	15	7	18	1	14	14	25

ADD PAIRS OF NUMBERS

CODETEXT	25	13	17	24	27	22	25	19	15	28	39

● When your agent decodes the message, he has to know that the key letter is q which is 17. He subtracts 17 from the first number of CODETEXT, so he gets $25 - 17 = 8$. He then subtracts the answer from the next number of CODETEXT and gets $13 - 8 = 5$. He keeps going until he has all the code numbers and he can swap them back into letters.

CODE TEXT	25	13	17	24	27
CODE LETTER	−17	−8	−5	−12	−12
=	8	5	12	12	15
PLAIN TEXT	h	e	l	l	o

27 MINUS 12 EQUALS...

Number grids

If you like number codes but think the a = 1 b = 2 system is a bit simple, you can do much better messages with a number grid like this one.

	1	2	3	4	5	6	7	8
10	TOM ORR OU	y	NO	q	7	NOW	u	h
20	K	CHEESE		YOU	2	C	O	DANGER
30		a	L	Ø	HELLO	Z	YELLOW	V
40	3	X	LOVE	b	t	BIR-MING-HAM	e	s
50	r	STOP	MARY POPP-INS		n	8	j	ATTACH
60	WHY	d	S		PANTS	S	GRANNY	P
70	i	GOR-GEOUS	1		M	100	6	KEY
80		9	g	SORRY		4	W	

Your grid can be any size. This one has 64 squares so there's plenty of room for the alphabet, the digits, and any words or phrases you tend to use a lot. Of course your agent would need a copy of this grid too, and it's a good idea to leave some boxes blank so you can fill them in with new words when you want them. Each box on the grid is coded by adding the number at the side to the number at the top, so the message "I love jam" would be 71 43 57 32 75. Of course once you've turned the messages into numbers, you can encode them to make them more secure.

Book code

Another way of putting a<5> message into numbers is to<10> use a book that you<15> and your agent both have<20> a copy of. Choose any<25> section you like and then<30> number each word. You'll see<35> this paragraph has got numbers<40> after every fifth word to<45> make them easier to count<50>.

Below is a message has been encoded using the above paragraph:

42 5 14 29 49 37 23 8 39 23 26.

If you give the message a sniff you might guess what it says, otherwise you can decode it one letter at a time. The first number is 42 so you find the 42nd word in the paragraph, which is "every," and write down the first letter "e." Then go on to find the 5th word and the 30th word and so on, and write down the first letters as you go.

Providing you and your agent keep the book you're using secret, this is an extremely secure code! That's just as well, as we wouldn't want too many people decoding that message and then taking it seriously.

PIG PENS

THIS CHAPTER SHOULD MAKE YOU FEEL RIGHT AT HOME!

You've already had a lot of math in this book and true Murderous Maths fans will be delighted to know that there are some really grim sums yet to come. But wouldn't it be sad if this book had told you all about the tough stuff and we left out one of the easiest bits? It's a bit like being able to solve sums like $397 \div 243 + 17 \cdot 264$ when you can't do $2 + 2$. You've got to be careful about being too clever as our uninvited visitors from the planet Zog are about to find out . . .

HAH! OUR COMPUTERS ARE NOW PROGRAMMED TO RECOGNISE AND EVALUATE EVERY LETTER FROM A-Z AND EVERY DIGIT FROM 0-9

OUR DATA BANKS CAN CHECK OVER ONE THOUSAND LANGUAGES AND SEVENTY THREE TRILLION DIFFERENT ENCRYPTION PATTERNS EVERY SECOND.

THERE IS NO HUMAN CODE WE CAN'T CRACK!

One of the cutest types of code is called a pig pen code. It uses signs rather than letters and here's one version. You can work out the signs you need from these diagrams.

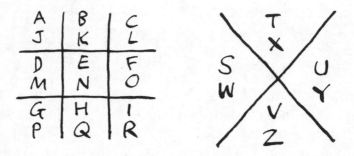

You choose the letter you want and draw the lines that appear round it. If the letter is the lower letter of the pair, put a dot in the middle of your sign. Here are the letters G and Y to show what's going on:

$$G = \daleth \qquad Y = \langle \cdot$$

Pig pen messages are great fun to draw and when you've finished they look nice and confusing.

The best part is that you and your agent can invent your own personalized pig pens. You just need to design one or more grids so that every position on it looks different. Here's another:

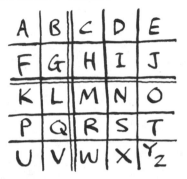

And of course pig pens are perfect if you're the sort of person who has got utterly fed up with computers taking over everything! It just goes to show that the best codes are not necessarily the most complicated ones.

DOUBLE CODES

Nearly all the messages we've seen involve one code and one key. You use the key to encode the message and your agent uses the same key to decode it. (When the same key is used for both jobs, it's called a *symmetric key*.) The problem is that at some point you need to give your agent the key. You could post it, chat about it, send it by carrier pigeon . . . and at that point if you're unlucky, the crackers will get to hear of it.

Wouldn't it be great to have a more clever key system?

To understand how these clever keys work, forget codes for a minute. Instead we'll pretend you've got a box that can be padlocked, and you have a padlock with two keys. You keep one key and put the other key in an envelope and post it to your agent.

Once your agent has got the key, you can send a message by putting it in the box and locking it with your key.

You then send the locked box to your agent who can unlock it.

But it's just like using codes because the weakness of the system comes when you send the key to your agent.

KEY COPYING MACHINE

Luckily you can stop this happening by using the double key system. The way to do this with padlocks is that you have one padlock with one key. Your agent has a different padlock with a different key. The crucial bit is that: *you never send each other a key. You don't even know what the other person's key looks like.*

Here's what happens:

This same system can work with two codes.

- You encode a message with your own private code (that nobody else knows) and send it to your agent.
- Your agent then encodes the coded message with his own code.
- The double-coded message is sent back to you.
- You decode your code and send it back to the agent.
- The agent decodes his code and can read the message.

Here's a very simple example. You want to send the message: "falling piano." You use a basic Caesar shift (see page 41) to change the letters with key letter = F and send this to your agent.

Your agent can't read the message, but codes it using the rail fence method (see page 26) and sends it back to you.

Now you decode it by reversing your Caesar shift and send it back:

Finally the agent can decode his code and get the message. . .

If you use double code, you must make absolutely sure that the two codes don't interfere with each other. Suppose you've got some mad woman called Janet who likes to encode numbers by adding 10 to them. To decode her number, she just takes 10 away. So if she starts with 20, she encodes it by doing $20 + 10 = 30$. To decode it, she works out $30 - 10 = 20$. Easy and foolproof. Her mad friend Wimton encodes and decodes numbers by multiplying then dividing by 5, so if he starts with 30 he gets $30 \times 5 = 150$ and then to decode he gets $150 \div 5 = 30$. Again no problems. But look what happens when they try to use double codes...

Janet starts with the number 20 and does $20 + 10 = 30$. She sends the answer to Wimton.

Wimton does $30 \times 5 = 150$ and he sends this back to Janet.

Janet then does $150 - 10 = 140$ and sends this to Wimton.

Wimton does $140 \div 5 = 28$.

You'll see 20 has turned into 28! This is because the two sums $+ 10$ and $\times 5$ interfered with each other, and in the wrong hands this can lead to disastrous consequences.

I MUST ADMIT, THIS DOUBLE CODE IS PRETTY GOOD! LET'S TRY IT.

Professor Fiendish and his pet pig Truffles both use different scrambling codes (see page 30). Truffles takes each pair of letters and swaps them round. The professor breaks the message into groups of three letters and reverses them. Ooh look—Truffles is sending a message already! (Can you see what she's saying?)

THE UNCRACKABLE CREDIT CARD CODE

At this point the book was supposed to finish, but here's what happened when it was delivered to the Murderous Maths headquarters.

140

Incidentally, we apologize if these pages of your book are a bit wet, but it's only a bit of bathwater. Mind you, when you see how murderous the math is, a few soggy bits of paper will be the least of your problems!

The RSA code
The brilliant code used to disguise credit card numbers in computers (and lots of other things) was invented in 1978 by Ron Rivest, Adi Shamir, and Leonard Adleman. If you put their initials together, you get RSA—which is the name of the code.

In terms of boxes and padlocks, their code works like this. You have one box, one padlock, and one key, but the trick is in the padlock. You have one of those padlocks that you can snap shut without having to turn a key; you only need a key to open it.

You can leave the box and the open padlock anywhere you like, and anyone can drop a message into it.

The person sending the secret message doesn't need your key, they just drop the message in the box, and snap the padlock shut.

Then they send you the locked box that no one else can open.

You unlock the box with the key.

Remember *anyone* can send you a message, but once the message is locked in the box, *nobody* else can read it, even the sender! This is why the RSA system is so good for buying shoes on the Internet. Anybody anywhere can use the code to send their credit card number, but nobody apart from the shoe shop can read it.

How does RSA help to buy shoes?

The RSA system uses two different keys (called *asymmetric keys*).

There is a **public key** to encode the message. This public key is made up of two numbers and they do the same job as the box and the open padlock. Anyone can use the public key to encode their message. Once encoded, they can't decode it.

There is also one completely different **private key** number that the shoe shop keeps very secret. They need this number to decode the message.

There are two tasty bits of math involved in the system, and to save putting big explanations in later, we'll explain them here. You can always skip this bit if you like.

● HUGE prime numbers (and we mean *really* huge). Prime numbers are numbers that only divide by themselves and 1. So 17 is prime because it won't divide by anything but 17 or 1. 18 is not prime because it divides by 18 and 1 but also 2, 3, 6, and 9. We'll be talking about prime numbers with hundreds of digits.

● Modular arithmetic. This is when you divide one number by another and all you care about is the remainder. For instance, 43 ÷ 8 = 5 with a remainder of 3. However if you see (43)MOD8, this means you do the same dividing sum but the answer is just 3 and you ignore the 5 completely. In the same way (22)MOD5 = 2 because 22 ÷ 5 = 4 with a remainder of 2. If you have a fancy calculator with a MOD button, try putting in 22 MOD 5 = and you should get the answer "2."

What makes the RSA code so good?

If you get any two prime numbers and multiply them together, the answer will only divide by those two numbers. For instance, 3 and 5 are both prime and 3 × 5 = 15. Nothing else apart from 3 and 5 will divide into 15 (apart from 15 and 1 of course, but they won't get you far). Multiplying any two numbers together to get an answer is easy. The real fun starts when you know the answer and you have to work backwards and find out what the two numbers were.

170,117 COMES FROM MULTIPLYING TWO PRIME NUMBERS TOGETHER

CAN YOU FIND OUT WHAT THEY ARE?

AW! THAT'S A REALLY MEAN QUESTION!

SNIGGER SNIGGER

We hope you didn't bother trying to work out the answer, but in case you did, the only possible result is 311 × 547 = 170,117.

The hardest RSA codes start with a prime number that's long enough fill the top half of this page, and it gets multiplied by another prime number that would fill the bottom half. The answer would fill a whole page! If you gave this answer to a computer, it would take a seriously long time to find the two prime numbers that made it.

BY THE TIME THE COMPUTER **DID** FIND THE ANSWERS...

THE UNIVERSE WILL PROBABLY HAVE COME TO AN END!

How to make the keys

If you want your agent (or anybody else) to send you a coded message, you have to start off by making a public key that involves two numbers we'll call **K** and **E**. You also need to make your private key, and this is just one number **D**. Stand by for some very fancy sums. . .

- First, you choose two prime numbers that we'll call **P** and **Q**. Although you're supposed to use HUGE prime numbers, to make things as simple as possible here we'll just use two small prime numbers so we'll say P = 3 and Q = 11.

- **K** = PQ, in other words you have to multiply P and Q together. Here we get P × Q = 3 × 11 = 33. So **K = 33.**

REMEMBER THAT K IS THE FIRST PART OF THE PUBLIC KEY.

- You then subtract 1 from each prime number and multiply the answers together. $(P - 1) \times (Q - 1) = 2 \times 10 = 20$. We'll call this number Florence, partly because it will always divide by four, but mainly because letters on their own are getting a bit dull.
- Now you can pick another number for **E**. There are a lot of special rules about choosing E, but as long as you choose a small prime number that doesn't divide into Florence you'll be fine. As 13 is a small prime number and it doesn't divide into 20, we'll choose it. So that's nice and easy, **E = 13**.

E IS THE SECOND PART OF THE PUBLIC KEY.

- Here's the tough bit. You have to work out **D** from this formula:

$$D = \frac{Z \times (P - 1)(Q - 1) + 1}{E}$$

You need to fiddle around with different values for Z until you get a whole number for D. We know that E = 13 and also $(P - 1)(Q - 1)$ is Florence, which is 20. If we put these in, we get:

$$D = \frac{Z \times 20 + 1}{13}$$

If we try making $Z = 1$, then on the top we'd get $1 \times 20 + 1 = 21$. When you try to divide 21 by 13, you don't get a whole number so that's no good. If Z was 2, the top would be $2 \times 20 + 1 = 41$ and this won't divide nicely by 13 either. If you keep going, you'll find that when $Z = 11$ you have more luck because $11 \times 20 + 1 = 221$, which DOES divide by 13. Yippee! So you just go ahead and divide 221 by 13, and the answer is 17. You've found **D = 17**!

- You only need K, E, and D so rip up, burn, and destroy P, Q, and Z, and send Florence away to somewhere nice where she'll be happy and nobody will turn up asking awkward questions.

What happens in real life

As soon as Miss Edwards wants to send her credit card number, the shoe shop computer goes through this whole process. In other words it picks two prime numbers and uses them to work out K and E that it sends to Miss Edwards's computer. It also works out D and keeps it to itself.

Remember that the prime numbers P and Q that the computer uses would normally be massive, so even if crackers knew what K and E were, they'd have no chance of working D out.

How to encode a message

WE'LL PRETEND THAT WE ARE MISS EDWARDS COMPUTER.

Once the shoe shop has sent the public key K = 33 and E = 13, Miss Edwards's computer can use these numbers to encode the number on her credit card.

She should relax—it's perfectly safe. Besides, the number on the card must be less than K and with the little prime numbers we've been using, K is only 33.

Here's the formula to encode the number (**A** is the number we're encoding and **C** is the encoded result):

- $C = (A^E) \mathrm{MOD} K$

We just put in the public key numbers: E = 13 and K = 33, and also we replace A with the credit card number, which is 27.

$$C = (27^{13}) \mathrm{MOD} 33$$

First we work out 27^{13} that comes to 4,052,555,153,018,976,267. Next we do the MOD33 bit, so we just divide it by 33 to see what the remainder is. If you work out 4,052,555,153,018,976,267 ÷ 33, you get 122,804,701,606,635,644 with a remainder of 15. The only bit we need is the 15, and that's the number encoded!

How to decode a message

When the coded message arrives, the shoe shop computer uses this formula:

- $A = (C^D) \bmod K$

The shop computer knows that $C = 15$ because that's what was sent by Miss Edwards's computer. The shop computer also knows $K = 33$ and D (the secret key) $= 17$ because it worked it out in the first place. The shop computer needs to find out A so it plonks the numbers in.

$A = (15^{17}) \bmod 33$

First the computer works out $15^{17} = 98,526,125,335,693,359,375$. Then it does the $\bmod 33$, which again means it has to divide by 33 and get the remainder. $98,526,125,335,693,359,375 \div 33 = 2,985,640,161,687,677,556$ with a remainder of 27.

And now for BIG numbers. . .

You've seen how RSA works with very small numbers. The primes were only 3 and 11, the coded number was just 27 and E was just 13. However you'll have noticed that the process produced numbers like 4,052,555,153,018,976,267 and 98,526,125,335,693,359,375. Impressed? Well don't be. These are just teeny compared to what really goes on.

If you do a bit of shopping on the Internet, your credit card might have a number such as 9876 5432 1012 3456. The first thing your computer does is convert it into a binary number of 1s and 0s, and the answer will generally end up with about 50 digits.

When your computer connects to the online store, their computer cooks up two prime numbers and produces the three numbers K, E, and D. It then forgets the prime numbers, it sends you K and E, and it keeps D very secret to itself.

Most computers have "128 bit encryption" these days—this means that the "K" number is 128 binary digits long!

Your computer then encodes your credit card with the $C = (A^E)$MODK formula, then sends the ecrypted number to the online store. Their computer works out $A = (C^D)$ MODK and gets your credit card number. Luckily computers have a few short cuts to working out MOD sums with binary numbers, but the numbers involved are still *gigantic* and that's what helps to keep a credit card number secret.